Anonymous

The Clapp Family Meeting at Northampton

August 1870

Anonymous

The Clapp Family Meeting at Northampton
August 1870

ISBN/EAN: 9783744692755

Printed in Europe, USA, Canada, Australia, Japan

Cover: Foto ©ninafisch / pixelio.de

More available books at **www.hansebooks.com**

THE

CLAPP FAMILY MEETING

AT NORTHAMPTON,

AUGUST 24, 1870.

COMPRISING

THE PROCEEDINGS, THE ADDRESS, HISTORICAL AND OTHER PAPERS, ETC.

PUBLISHED BY VOTE OF THE BOSTON COMMITTEE OF ARRANGEMENTS.

BOSTON:
EBENEZER CLAPP, 7 SCHOOL STREET.
OTIS CLAPP, 3 BEACON STREET.

Printed by DAVID CLAPP & SON, 334 Washington Street.
1870.

Boston, September 1, 1870.

THE Boston Committee of Arrangements for the late meeting of the Clapp Family at Northampton, in consequence of the difficulty of convening the general Committee, do hereby, for themselves, and in behalf, as they believe, of all who attended that most pleasant and successful re-union, offer their sincere thanks:—

First, to their Connecticut River kindred, who inaugurated the movement and who so laboriously and prosperously aided in carrying it forward.

Second, to the Rev. Charles A. Humphreys, of Springfield, for his fervent invocation, at the opening of the meeting, of the Divine blessing upon the assembly and the proceedings of the day.

Third, to William D. Clapp, Esq., of Northampton, for his very appropriate and friendly words of welcome.

Fourth, to Hon. Almon M. Clapp, the President of the Day, for his fraternal and animated opening remarks, and for the very acceptable manner in which he performed the duties of presiding officer.

Fifth, to the Rev. Alexander H. Clapp, D.D., for his eloquent, instructive and entertaining Address; and

Sixth, to the other gentlemen who contributed to the interest and importance of the meeting by written papers, and speeches; and the Committee respectfully solicit for the press a copy of each of the productions alluded to.

They also appoint the Chairman of this meeting, with three other gentlemen to be selected by him, as a Committee to transmit a copy of this vote to the gentlemen named, and to attend to the publication, if they shall find sufficient encouragement, of the Proceedings at this the first Family Gathering of the Clapps.

[The Committee thus appointed consisted of EBENEZER CLAPP (Chairman), OTIS CLAPP, DAVID CLAPP and WILLIAM CLAPP.]

To EBENEZER, OTIS, DAVID AND WILLIAM CLAPP, COMMITTEE.

DEAR KINSMEN:

I gratefully acknowledge your note, conveying the thanks of the Committee of Arrangements for my Address at Northampton, and their request of a copy for the press. Herewith you have the manuscript.

None can be better aware than the writer, of its many imperfections. It was prepared, at your desire, for the entertainment of a passing hour at our late Re-union, and with no thought of further use. I had not before been specially interested in our genealogy; had no time for research; and, excepting the manuscript "annals" of our Historian, no materials not open to all. Nor have I since had leisure to put into presentable shape, matter that answered its purpose tolerably, when spoken in the indulgent hearing of "the family." But, remembering that it is to be printed, not for "the public," but for the same partial kinsfolk, I will not alter even its familiar, colloquial form, nor apologize for its evident incompleteness as an historical document.

Doubtless many of our kindred have lived and died, as worthy of honorable mention as most of those named in the Address—named, because the facts concerning them were more easily found.

The hope that this fragmentary attempt may draw from their obscurity materials for a fuller and juster tribute, in the forthcoming "Family History," makes me willing to give these pages to the printer. And if thus they shall fall under "the critic's eye," let him remember that they were not prepared for his entertainment, but for that of a proverbially indulgent Family.

Ever,

Faithfully yours,

ALEXANDER HUNTINGTON CLAPP.

Bible House, New York, Oct. 1, 1870.

CLAPP FAMILY MEETING.

INTRODUCTORY.

In the year 1858, several members of the Clapp Family in Boston, impressed with the desirableness of assembling together as many of the name and lineage as could be induced to meet in one place, made an effort to bring about such a gathering in the town of Dorchester, the venerated home of their first American progenitors. At a meeting of these individuals, several of whom were on the Boston Committee for the Family Gathering of 1870, it was unanimously voted to invite the Rev. Theodore Clapp, of New Orleans, to deliver an Address on the occasion proposed. On account of the state of his health, to their great regret he declined, in a very friendly and appropriate letter, dated Oct. 8, 1858. They subsequently invited the Rev. George Putnam, D.D., of Roxbury, Mass., a lineal descendant on the maternal side, who after taking the matter into consideration, declined, in a letter of May 13, 1859. The Rev. Dr. Furness, of Philadelphia, also a member of the family, likewise declined the invitation. Soon after the time last mentioned, several of the aged and more prominent men of the name in Dorchester died, which served to throw discouragement on the efforts for the contemplated meeting.

Another obstacle in the way, was the want of suitable accommodations in the town named, for the numerous progeny whom it was hoped would congregate around their ancestral homestead and near the sepulchres of their fathers. The effort was therefore abandoned for the time-being—but not forgotten.

Early the present year a desire for a similar family gathering sprung up in the minds of some of the Connecticut River kindred. Other families, of different names, but of the same old Puritan stock, had recently met together, and accounts of their fraternal and joyous greetings had excited in the community generally an increased love of ancestry and kindred, and encouraged the effort for other family re-unions. Mr. Joel T. and Mr. Moses Clapp, of Southampton, Mass., first conferred together with regard to calling a meeting of the Clapp Family somewhere in that neighborhood. A consultation was held with others in the vicinity, several meetings were convened, and a Committee of twelve from various towns was appointed to consider the whole subject. This Committee was afterwards enlarged, and comprised the following persons:

William D. Clapp, William R. Clapp, Charles C. Clapp, Henry S. Gere, *Northampton;* Joel Taylor Clapp, Moses Clapp, Stephen D. Clapp, Jr., *Southampton;* R. Wright Clapp, *Westhampton;* Theodore Clapp, William N. Clapp, Lewis Clapp, A. S. Ludden, *Easthampton;* Dr. H. W. Clapp, E. M. Clapp, *Westfield;* Rev. Lewis F. Clark, *Whitinsville;* Franklin Clapp, Elnathan Graves, *Williamsburg;* Sylvanus Clapp, *Pawtucket, R. I.;* James H. Clapp, *Belchertown;* Robinson Clapp, *Holyoke;* Otis, Ebenezer, David, William, William Warland, and John Codman Clapp, *Boston;* Lewis Clapp, *Lee Centre, Ill.;* Dr. A. B. Clapp, *Aurelius, N. Y.;* Rev. Luther Clapp, *Wauwatosa, Wis.;* Russel Clapp, *Swan Township, Ind.;* Seth C. Clapp, *Princeton, Ill;* Caleb Clapp, *Hartford, Conn.;* Spencer Clapp, *Windsor, Conn.;* George M. Clapp, *Newburgh, N. Y.*

LAFAYETTE CLAPP, *Secretary.*

At a meeting, March 3d, it was voted expedient to call the proposed family gathering. A correspondence had taken place with some of the name in Boston, who were invited to meet at Easthampton with their western kindred, and confer upon the best method of carrying out the plan; and at an adjourned meeting held on the 18th of April, Messrs. Ebenezer and Otis Clapp, of Boston, were accordingly present. At that meeting, a Sub-Committee on Speakers was appointed, consisting of Ebenezer, Otis and William N. Clapp. Also a Committee on Place of Meeting, consisting of Moses, Charles C., Dr. H. W., Lewis, and Oliver N. Clapp. A Committee of Invitation was also chosen: viz., Theodore and Lafayette Clapp, of Easthampton, and H. W. Clapp, of Westfield, who issued a general circular to the family and its connections. A Committee was afterwards appointed on the Collation, as follows:—Theodore and Lewis Clapp of Easthampton, William D. and William R. Clapp of Northampton, and Joel Taylor Clapp of Southampton. These various Committees made arrangements which resulted in the choice of the Agricultural Grounds in Northampton as the place, and the 24th of August as the time of holding the proposed meeting; and also in securing the services of the Hon. Almon M. Clapp, of

Washington, D. C., as President of the Day, and of the Rev. Alexander H. Clapp, D.D., of New York City, as Orator for the occasion.

On the 20th of July, notice was sent out by the Boston Committee, of a meeting of all interested, to be held at the house of Mr. William Clapp, in Boston, on the 1st of August. At that meeting, the following gentlemen were appointed to make arrangements for railroad conveyance of all who might wish to go from Boston and its vicinity: viz., Otis, William, Eugene H., Lemuel and Charles M. Clapp. This Committee made an agreement on favorable terms with the Boston & Albany and the Connecticut River Railroads to convey the party to and from the place of meeting; also with the proprietors of Haynes's Hotel, in Springfield, for accommodations the first night, and issued a circular, containing the necessary information, dated August 18th.

On the 24th, a party of more than one hundred left Boston in the afternoon, and reached Springfield early in the evening. After tea, a social gathering was held in the spacious parlors of the hotel, at which were present, besides the Boston and Dorchester party, many of the Connecticut River and other members of the family, some of them from distant parts of the country.

Of this meeting, none who were present will consider any terms of praise too extravagant. One of the reporters present speaks of "the cordiality, good fellowship and freedom from formality which marked the assemblage." Another says, "The rooms presented quite a busy scene, filled with the young and old, their faces beaming with smiles as they greeted old acquaintances, and added fraternal links to the chain of friendship." A prominent member of the family who was present, writes, since his return home, "I shall not, during all my earthly pilgrimage, forget the delightful season spent with friends at Springfield and Northampton. It will long be remembered among the most delightful scenes of my life. It was good to be there." Another writes, from his distant residence, "We are highly pleased that we had sense enough to accept the invitation to this most happy and interesting gathering, which gave us so much pleasure, and which will be remembered and alluded to, in coming years, as one of the most agreeable incidents of our lives. I say *we*, for my wife enjoyed the whole affair as much as any one, and has proved herself to have the qualities which, I think, make some of the Clapps clever people. I hope my good Dorchester friends will be willing to admit her into full communion as an unabridged, unmitigated Clapp." Another, a lady not so far from the old ancestral home, writes, "Gathered together for the first time under one roof, and meeting various branches from other and distant points, it was a most interesting and delightful occasion. Dear to all our hearts will be the memory of this our first family re-union. The spacious rooms were thronged with young and old—some were acquaintances and friends, but most were strangers to each other. Some were brought together once more whom scores of years had separated, and many a warm and cordial grasp of the hand was exchanged. Some who had known each other by name only, here met face to face. Others, whose homes were perhaps in the same city or town, knew of each other here for the first time. Thus by the strengthening of old acquaintance, and the formation of new and kindlier feelings towards all, both friends and strangers, the bond of brotherhood was made stronger. And then our thoughts almost instinctively went back to the past—to good old Roger Clap and his brethren. What would he say to us here to-night—to us his children even to the eighth generation—thus brought together in the midst of the knowledge, prosperity and cultivation that belong to our age and country? And would he not have found that a feeling of veneration existed beneath the cheerful, social spirit of this family band? It *was* this spirit of fond remembrance of the Past, and of our fathers who lived in it, that penetrated and pervaded the happy meeting. It was this that brightened the countenance of each towards all, and joined them indeed into one brotherly kindred. At its close there was a solemnity amounting almost to awe, as with one accord the social festival was succeeded by the music and song of Auld Lang Syne; and higher still both thought and feeling were carried up in a hymn of praise to Him who presides over all the families of the earth, and has watched over and blessed our house and lineage for these long generations."

Among the interesting incidents of the evening was the passing around for inspection of several old relics of the family. Deacon Ebenezer Clapp, of Dorchester, showed a watch whose history was told by the following inscription on parchment inside:—

This watch was the property of Rev. Nathaniel Clapp, of Newport, R. I., who was born in 1668, and died in 1745, aged 77 years. At his death it was valued at twenty pounds—$88.80.

Derastus Clapp also exhibited a copper plate for printing clock dials, which had been the property of his grandfather, Preserved Clapp. It is a fine specimen of engraving, and was probably executed in England.

On the morning of the 24th, the party from Boston, with others resident in Springfield and its vicinity and from more distant places, were conveyed over the Connecticut River Railroad to Northampton, and by means of omnibuses and other conveyances soon reached the grounds of the Hampshire County Agricultural Society. The large hall of the Society had been prepared for the occasion, and by 10 o'clock between five and six hundred people had gathered in it. This number was much increased subsequently, till nearly or quite one thousand had collected within the hall or were standing by the open windows outside. Before the exercises began, a paper prepared for the purpose, designed to contain the names, parentage, &c., of those present, was circulated for signatures.

After the meeting had been called to order by THEODORE CLAPP, Esq., of Easthampton, a fervent and impressive Prayer was offered by Rev. CHARLES A. HUMPHREYS, of Springfield, a native of Dorchester, and a lineal descendant of Nicholas Clapp.

The following Hymn, written by Rev. Dr. James Flint for a public occasion many years since, was now sung to the tune of "Old Hundred" by the large audience, nearly all joining in the inspiring strain:—

IN pleasant lands have fallen the lines
That bound our goodly heritage,
And safe beneath our sheltering vines
Our youth is blest, and soothed our age.

What thanks, O God, to Thee are due,
That Thou didst plant our fathers here;
And watch and guard them as they grew,
A vineyard, to the Planter dear.

The toils they bore, our ease have wrought;
They sowed in tears—in joy we reap;
The birthright they so dearly bought
We'll guard, till we with them shall sleep.

Thy kindness to our fathers shown,
In weal and wo, through all the past,
Their grateful sons, O God, shall own,
While here their name and race shall last.

The assembly was then addressed by WILLIAM D. CLAPP, Esq., of Northampton, in the following words of welcome:—

To all here present who bear the honored name of Clapp, or who are either directly or remotely connected with the lineage, we bring, this morning, words of cordial welcome. Pride of birth, of race, of lineage, may be one of the frailties and foibles of human nature, but if so it is at least a pardonable weakness.

Ridicule as we may the chivalrous sentiment that takes note of and holds in high honor a genealogy that runs back through successive generations into the centuries of the past, in a greater or less degree to that sentiment we are all loyal, and it is the inspiring motive that has led to this goodly gathering to-day.

We are not so presumptuous as to claim descent from lords or thrones, though, for aught we know, could some "Old Mortality" unveil the lost records of the past, our line might perchance be found to be crossed by royal blood. However that may be, we are proud of our ancestors and our history. The main progenitors of the race have left a noble record of their days. They have left their impress on the sands of time. We cherish their memory to-day, and are glad that so many of our name are now here. We are proud of our descent, and we have an interest in the good deeds of our ancestors, which give us a right to be proud of them and regard them with high honor.

In issuing our call for this first gathering of the family, we have, in the language of Scripture, said "to the North, Give up! and to the South, Keep not back; bring my sons from far and my daughters from the ends of the earth."

Right nobly have you responded to the call, and to-day we greet friends massed from all parts of the country.

In conclusion, he said he extended to them the right hand of fellowship. The time was theirs, sacred to the past, and he knew they would properly improve it. If they might judge by the proof there to-day, the race was not likely soon to die out.

The Hon. ALMON M. CLAPP, of Washington, D. C., was then introduced, and spoke as follows:—

KINDRED AND FRIENDS:

YOU have honored me over-much upon this occasion, and in responding to this expression of your wish and esteem, I will appropriate a sentence from the late lamented and martyred Lincoln, when he was honored with a re-nomination for the Presidency: "I will neither conceal my gratification nor restrain the expression of my gratitude" that this large gathering of my kindred and blood should have deemed me not unworthy to preside over your deliberations. In accepting this high honor, I am impressed with emotions that are not readily expressed in language. In consideration of this mark of your partiality, I am led incontinently to inquire, why, when all New England teems with the name and blood of our ancestors, am I selected for this honor? Why is a mere nomad of the race—one whose *pater familias* isolated him from the scenes of his New England nativity even in the hours of his childhood, and whose lot has been cast towards the setting sun during most of the remainder of his days, now selected for this distinctive honor? My friends, in seeking a solution of this problem, I am led to attribute your kind action either to that high toned spirit of courtesy which has characterized the people of New England since the feet of our ancestors first pressed its soil; or to that noble Christian prompting of the human heart, which, according to holy tradition, sacrificed the fatted calf when the prodigal son returned to the paternal roof after a period of protracted and painful separation. Let the prompting influence of your action be what it may, I am not insensible to the honor conferred, or to the responsibilities that follow in its train.

It may not be improper, my friends, to tender hearty thanks to that representative of our scattered family who conceived the happy thought that has led to this delightful re-union, in which we are permitted to see each other face to face, form new acquaintances, and lengthen and strengthen the chain of personal friendship. Neither is it unbecoming the occasion that we should devoutly return thanks to "Our Father who art in Heaven," for having spared our lives that we, here assembled, may share the enjoyments of this pleasant and highly interesting occasion.

My friends, we meet to-day as kindred, bearing the blood of a name, which, though it may never yet have been recorded high as others upon the column of this world's fame, has seldom, if ever, been tarnished by dishonor or tainted by crime. And though it shall appear, that, as a kindred people, we have shared less of what the world counts honorable distinction, we are fully compensated in the reflection that we are in no degree subject to the feelings of shame and mortification which are excited by a sense of popular or private disgrace.

If, in the course of human events, we have acted less prominently on the stage where the more honored distinctions of worldly fame are contended for and won, we have had the more time to devote to the industrial pursuits and avocations of life, where personal integrity and usefulness challenge respect, and where "the post of honor is the private station."

I congratulate you, my friends and kindred, on this auspicious gathering. We are of a distinct blood and ancestry. Here—

"Heart leaps to heart; the sacred flood
  That warms us is the same.
Those good old men—their honest blood
  Alike we fondly claim.

Our boyish sports were all the same,
  Each little joy and woe—
Let manhood keep alive the flame,
  Lit up so long ago."

Though this is our first family gathering, may it not be our last. Though it is the beginning, may a kind Providence decree that these re-unions shall be perpetuated and properly observed by ourselves, our children and our children's children, to the remotest generation.

We have met here to-day, my friends, not to commemorate deeds of heroic daring. We come not to contemplate and rejoice over a nation's triumphs, or to deplore its defeats and disasters. We come not to consider the interests of agriculture, commerce, manufactures, education or religion. We come not to review the bloody scenes of the old world. But we come as kindred, in whose veins courses the same blood.

We come as brothers, sisters, friends, and let us "keep the link that binds us, bright!"

In coming together on this venerated spot, this beautiful portion of our beloved country—in this delightful town of Northampton—where so many of our kindred dwell, surrounded by the evidences of God's highest munificence—where these noble old elms beckon us to their vernal shades—we meet on classic ground. There flows the venerable Connecticut, whose sylvan retreat inspired the muse of Brainard when he so sweetly and devoutly sang:—

"Stream of my sleeping fathers! when the sound
Of coming war echoed the hills around,
How did they then start forth from every glade,
Snatching the musket where they left the spade.
How did their mothers urge them to the fight,
Their sisters tell them to defend the right.
How bravely did they stand—how nobly fall,
The earth their coffin and the turf their pall!
How did the aged pastor light his eye
When to his flock he read with purpose high
And stern resolve, whate'er the toil may be,
To pledge life, name, fame, all, for liberty."

We assemble here to-day as the representatives of genuine personal worth, impressed with memories that bring no regrets, save that time has removed our ancestors from the scenes of their earthly usefulness, and that the places which once knew them will know them no more forever. Their graves and the memories that cluster around them are their monuments; and as we wander among and point to their resting-places with emotions of just family pride, we are led to exclaim with Percival:—

"Here rest the great and good. Here they repose
After their generous toil. A sacred band,
They take their sleep together, while the year
Comes with its early flowers to deck their graves
And gather them again as winter frowns.
Theirs is no vulgar sepulchre—green sods
Are all their monument, and yet it tells
A nobler history than pillared piles,
Or eternal pyramids. They need
No statue, nor inscription, to reveal
Their greatness. It is around them, and the joy
With which their children tread the hallowed ground
That holds their venerated bones, the peace
That smiles on all they fought for, and the wealth
That clothes the land they rescued; these, though mute,
As feeling ever is when deepest—these
Are monuments more lasting than the fanes
Reared by the kings and demigods of old."

But I must forbear. I have already trespassed too long upon your time and patience by detaining you from an intellectual banquet that is spread and awaits your grateful enjoyment. Pardon this interference with your pleasure, and grant me your further generous indulgence, while I proceed with the duties of a position which I accept with emotions of profound gratitude.

The President then introduced the Rev. ALEXANDER HUNTINGTON CLAPP, of New York City, who delivered the following Address.

ADDRESS.

My Kinsmen, Honored and Beloved:

If we are asked why we are here to-day, let us say, "Because blood is thicker than water." We say it not with the old feudal notion that "the blue blood of nobility," flowing through a long line of titled idlers, oppressors and extortioners, nourishes a superior life, confers diviner rights, demands a more obsequious recognition from the untitled many: but thus asserting our faith that by God's appointment the bond of kindred is a sacred reality; community of ancestry is a chord that, deftly struck, vibrates through hearts widely severed by time, distance, difference of calling, culture, experience, and even of faith; opens the common fount of sympathy with personal and household joys and sorrows, suffuses the cheek with shame at frailty, and uplifts the heart with pride in noble achievement, with which are linked our common name.

We have not met for self-glorification—to claim that this family has been learned, virtuous, honored or useful, above other families of the land whose glory is its intelligent virtuous households. Enough for us, if we shall find that those who have borne and are bearing our name have not been behind other kindreds, in whose prosperity and welfare we will rejoice as if they were our own.

It will be natural for us—will it not be the gratification of a proper curiosity and interest?—to look back a little at the origin

2

and history of the family. Of course only the briefest hints are possible in an address like this, and nothing more will be attempted than the roughest sketch of a few of the more prominent features. The time will allow of scarcely an allusion to the many other honored names linked with ours by marriage; nor, for obvious reasons, can we say much of the living. It may fairly be supposed that they are here to speak for themselves!

For the more thorough and elaborate collection of the facts of our history, in a form for permanent preservation, fortunately we are blessed with a Family Historian, whom you all should know—Deacon Ebenezer Clapp, of the Dorchester Antiquarian Society. Elisha Clapp, of Boston, assisted by Charles Clapp, of Bath, Me., spent some twenty-five years in collecting material, which was made over to Deacon Ebenezer; and he, since 1840, has given much hard labor and no little money to the carrying forward of the work. For these more than sixty years of toil, research and correspondence, all who bear the name are under weighty obligations; and this meeting, I submit, ought not to dissolve without taking measures for the publication of the body of family history in our cousin Ebenezer's possession, before fire or some other casualty shall destroy it.

I make no secret of the fact that, though I have not neglected other sources, for by far the most of the statements to follow, the Family Historian—as I shall call Mr. Ebenezer Clapp—is my authority. What he does not know of the Clapp tribe can be of little account; and I profess to act mainly as his mouthpiece, to set before you facts which his research, chiefly, has made it possible thus succinctly to rehearse. If then there shall be any thing in this address worth hearing, credit it to him; its crudities and imperfections are all my own.

The family name, variously spelled in the old English annals, is Saxon, and is easily traced back to one for whom the parish of Clapham (the home of Clapp), in Surrey, was named, in the time of "Edward the Confessor."

And now I do hope none of you have heard the news: for it is such an honor to be the first to tell you that—*like all* our American Republican families that trace back their lineage—*we are of noble descent!* Mark that! The Historian has had faithfully painted, and will show to you who are interested, the family "coat of arms"—of which this is the excellent legend: "Cassis tutissima Virtus" (Virtue is the safest helmet), and this is the heraldic description: "He bearth Sable A Lion Read in Camp Black spoted with goold, A Hair and a Gray houn in ful speed in green Camp, spoted with goold, Betwen a Chueron Black Boarder'd with goold, by y[e] name of Richard Clap Earl of Hampton." The Earl of Hampton! We see now how natural it was that the early Clapps should take so kindly to these clustering Hamptons of the *New* England.

The present audience will be interested chiefly in the story of the family, since its settlement in this country.

Five men of our name were among the early settlers of New England—Capt. ROGER, of blessed memory; Deacon EDWARD, his brother; and their three cousins, THOMAS, NICHOLAS and JOHN—all of whom came to Dorchester, which has from the first been the chief seat of the Clapps—Northampton must take the second place—and seems to glory in the fact. Besides these, one of the name (spelling it with a K), came from Germany to Philadelphia, some time in the seventeenth century, and has descendants at the South and West. But the great body of the thousands now bearing the name in the United States, are descended from the first four just named; most of these Northampton Clapps being of the blood of Capt. Roger, through his son, Preserved.

And though but few words can be given to any, even the worthiest of our ancestors; though many most excellent will not even be named, you will insist on a tribute of grateful love and veneration to this heroic and saintly man. Fortunately the chief facts of his life were recorded by his own quaint, truthful pen, in a little volume that has been several times reprinted—

last, by the faithful care of our Family Historian, under the auspices of the Dorchester Antiquarian Society. The book should never be out of print, so long as there are those of our name to reverence exalted virtue.

CAPTAIN ROGER CLAP.

ROGER CLAP, son of Richard, was born at Salcombe, in Devonshire, England, in 1609; his father being, as he says, "A man fearing God, and in good esteem among God's faithful servants, with an outward estate not great—I think not above £80 per annum." Roger came to America with the first settlers of Dorchester, in 1630, arriving on the 30th of May, after a passage of ten weeks. In the great scarcity of bread the new-comers subsisted mainly on fish till supplies could be had from abroad, and the first crops grown. Our ancestor was fortunate enough to have a father able and willing to send supplies, greatly to his relief and that of the colony.

I will here go no further into the *motive* for his coming, than to say—what the most cursory reader of his autobiography will see for himself—that Roger Clap was a Pilgrim of the Pilgrims. The temptation is great, to go here into a eulogy of the New-England Pilgrim branch of the grand old heroic Puritan stock; for I verily believe that the earth never saw nobler spirits than those same Pilgrims. But trusting that there is not one here who does not honor them, and knowing that our kinsman, Otis Clapp, of Boston, is to speak of them shortly, I forbear. Enough to say, that our sturdy old ancestor was one of the purest and most goodly of them all.

He could find little food for his hungry soul in the established church, as it then was, and even in his boyhood left his father's home for a neighboring town, that he might be under the spiritual care of the pious pastor, Warham, with whom and the devout Maverick he came over the sea and coöperated in the church of Dorchester, of which he was a member for sixty years.

He married Johanna Ford, one of his fellow immigrants, in

her seventeenth year—he being in his twenty-fifth. They had ten sons and four daughters, of whom but four sons and two daughters lived to become heads of families. His repute among the discerning people of Dorchester is seen in the fact that they very early gave him command of their militia, chose him to represent the town in the General Court, and authorized him to join persons in marriage—neither of which trusts were in those days reposed in any persons not of known excellence of character. In 1665 he was, by appointment of the General Court, put in command of "the Castle," in Boston harbor, the chief fortress of the Province—now Fort Independence. This post of peculiar trust and honor, he held for twenty-one years. Cotemporary history says that he enlisted only pious as well as brave men for the Castle; that he treated them with affectionate kindness, watching for their religious welfare and making the Castle for them a happy Christian home. "In his time," says one of his biographers, "it might be seen that religious and well-disposed men might take upon them the calling of a soldier without hurting their morals or their good name."

The Captain resided with his family in the Castle, and maintained worship there, but faithfully attended Sunday and week-day religious services in Dorchester and Boston—in all things a pattern and helper to his family and the garrison.

An incident is recorded which shows the general love and esteem for Captain Roger. Being visited in the Castle with a fit of sickness, the good people of Dorchester "united in a day of fasting and prayer for his recovery;" and when God mercifully restored him, "they observed a day of thanksgiving."

In 1686, when, as Blake says, "by the loss of our charter there was a change of government, and some things were required of him that were grievous to his pious soul"—"unwilling to lend his coöperation to the tyrannical schemes of Gov. Andros," says the historian of Dorchester—"and foreseeing a storm of troubles coming on the country, and he now in his old age [77 years], he voluntarily resigned his command." About four years after his resignation, he died, Feb. 2, 1690–1, in the

82d year of his age, and was buried in the "King's Chapel" ground in Boston, with no little honor for those days—the military, the Governor and the whole General Court attending, and marching to the solemn music of the Castle guns. His wife followed him, in 1695, aged 78.

The account of Capt. Clap and his family, written by James Blake, Jr., author of Blake's Annals, who rightly describes himself as "one that was acquainted therewith," says of the Captain: "He had great aversion to idleness, and made conscience of employing himself about some lawful business; was a hearty lover of his country, prayed often for it; was chiefly concerned that pure Religion should flourish here; he encouraged the good and discountenanced the evil; was meek and humble, yet of uncommon intellectual and spiritual gifts; of cheerful, pleasant disposition, courteous and kind, free and familiar in his conversation, yet with a proper reservedness, and a gravity and presence that commanded respect from others."

Can we not all, in view of this shining Christian life, heartily unite with the prayer of Blake: "May the blessing of those godly ancestors rest upon their posterity, even unto the latest generations! And may their posterity put themselves in the way to inherit these blessings, by continuing steadfast in the covenant of their God, under which their ancestors have brought them, and by walking in and cleaving to the good ways of their forefathers, treading in their steps and making good their ground!"

Captain Roger's brother, Edward, his three cousins—Thomas, Nicholas and John—with his two sisters (wives of George Weeks and Nicholas Clap), all came to this country by his advice—Edward, Thomas and Nicholas in 1633, John later, probably in 1637; all settled in and near Dorchester, and were men of mark in their day. All except John left children; he adopted the town of Dorchester as his heir, bequeathing to it (after the death of his widow) sixteen acres of land, which years afterwards sold for $1,000 an acre, "for the support of the ministry and of a school forever." I cannot attempt even the roughest sketch of these men, but you will expect a few words concerning them.

Deacon EDWARD, elder brother of Capt. Roger, died in 1664, having served the town of Dorchester in many of its most responsible offices, and been deacon of the church for twenty-six years. He left nine children, and a good name as an enterprising, honest man, rich in good will and good deeds.

His wife was a sister of Thomas, Nicholas and John.

THOMAS, cousin of Capt. Roger, was born in Dorchester, England, in 1597, came to *our* Dorchester in 1633, removed to Weymouth, thence, before 1640, to Scituate, where many have since borne the name. His descendants are probably more numerous than those of either of the others. He died in 1684, aged 87. He had been thirty-seven years a deacon, was a deputy to the General Court, and a staunch defender of the faith (as he understood it), against all "pestilent heresies" on the one hand, and spiritual tyranny on the other. He was deep in the thirty-three years' war in Scituate, on the subject of Baptism, which commenced under the ministry of Mr. (afterwards President) Chauncey, and was one of the three messengers of peace that at last brought about a reconciliation.

Of Thomas's sons, Samuel long represented the town in General Court, was Commissioner to settle boundaries, and held other responsible positions.

Eleazer was killed in the famous battle with the Narragansetts, March, 1676, when sixty-three out of seventy whites and friendly Indians were killed.

NICHOLAS, brother of Thomas, whose wife was sister of Capt. Roger and Edward, was also a deacon and town officer for many years, and was esteemed "a most valuable man." He died in Dorchester, 1679.

His daughter, Hannah, was fortunate enough, in 1688, to marry Ebenezer Strong, of Northampton, and they were the great-great-grandparents of Gov. Caleb Strong. Her cousin, Esther, daughter of Deacon Edward, had married, in 1684, Samuel, brother of Ebenezer Strong, and they were the grandparents of Hon. Simeon Strong, Judge of the Supreme Court of Massachusetts.

This audience needs no reminder of the honor in which the name of Strong has been justly held.

This Nicholas was the ancestor of our Historian, Ebenezer, and of the more than thirty families now bearing our name in Dorchester. If our Historian were not here, or were not a man of such maidenly modesty, I would for a moment forget that he is one of "the living." As it is, I shall say a word of his father —and Dorchester people do say that *our* Ebenezer is very much *like* his father.

Ebenezer (the father) was the *eighth* Deacon Clap in the Dorchester church. He carried on a large farm and tannery; in which *our* Ebenezer, born in 1809, helped him until he went into the Boston Custom-House, in 1831, and afterwards into the book trade and work upon the family annals. The father was selectman eleven years, school committee fifteen years, town representative, a volunteer in the time of Shay's rebellion, &c. He died, 1860, in his 89th year.

Our Historian's mother was Eunice, daughter of John Pierce, of Dorchester, and died in 1849. His father again married, and his widow, long known as the "Dorchester beauty," died in 1864. Both father and mother are spoken of as models of old-style courtesy and kindness, as well as of genuine piety—which may account for some traits in our honored Historian!

The elder Ebenezer's unmarried sister, Lucy, was for years a private teacher in Dorchester, and from her Alexander H. and Edward Everett learned their "a b abs"—which may account for some things in *their* later career!

It was our Ebenezer's uncle, Deacon John, of Roxbury, whom Dr. George Putnam (a descendant of the first Deacon Edward) called "the last of the Puritans," "one who embodied in himself all that was respectable and lovely in the primitive worthies of New England." "A plain downright man, yet affable and courteous, who never did a thing for show, had none of the restless pride of life, and gave the world the spectacle of a calm, cheerful, blameless, contented old age."—Some knowing people say that when *our* Ebenezer gets to be an old man, this portrait will answer for him!

CAPTAIN ROGER'S CHILDREN.

Of the fourteen children of Capt. Roger, eight died young, and six died in a good old age—ranging between 66 and 74 years. These six were Samuel, Elizabeth, Preserved, Hopestill, Wait, and Desire. They are *all* said to have been persons of more than ordinary ability and influence; all lived and died in the vicinity of Boston and Dorchester, except Elder PRESERVED, born 1643, who had the kind consideration for many of us to come—keeping a sharp lookout for Indian arrows and rifles on the way—to Northampton with a Dorchester colony and found the First Church; then to fall in love with and marry the beautiful, rich and accomplished Sarah Newberry, then seventeen years old, the daughter of one of the chief rulers of Connecticut—Benjamin Newberry, for twenty-two sessions a Representative, and a Captain in King Philip's war. But for this wise forethought of Elder Preserved, and for the fact that he was so good a shot, and pious enough to keep his powder dry when treacherous Indians practised on him for a target, I dare say the Committee would have called this meeting to-day somewhere else than in Northampton, and some of us would decidedly have failed of an invitation. As it is, this town, the neighboring Hamptons, and other towns of western Massachusetts, Vermont, Connecticut, and elsewhere, can bear witness that our good old ancestor experienced the blessing of "the man who hath his quiver full of them." Of their children, seven grew to maturity. One of them, Thomas, moved to Hartford, and is the ancestor of most of our name in Connecticut.

Here in Northampton, Elder Preserved died in 1720, aged 77, after having been for many years Captain, Representative in General Court, and Ruling Elder in the church. All of the three brothers were Representatives and Ruling Elders, and Preserved and Samuel were also Captains. And this, remember, at a time when such appointments meant that their fellow-citizens believed them to be true, brave, honest, godly men.

The two daughters of Capt. Roger also were married, and were both blessed in their pious husbands and children.

Desire, the youngest of Capt. Roger's sons who lived to manhood, also married in Dorchester, "was a sober and religious man," and trained up four children, who walked worthily in his steps.

Without attempting to follow direct lines of descent, we pass now to brief notices of a few of the family who had in their day more than ordinary prominence—beginning with the Clergy, for of them the fullest records are left.

REV. THOMAS CLAP, PRESIDENT OF YALE COLLEGE.

THOMAS, great-grandson of Thomas of Scituate, and son of Dea. Stephen and Temperance, was born in Scituate, 1703, fitted for College with Rev. James McSparrow, English missionary to the Narragansetts, entered Harvard at the age of 15, and graduated in 1722.

He ascribes his deep religious experience to a treatise of Mr. Stoddard of Northampton, read while in college, and which decided him to enter the ministry, "because," he says, "I apprehended that in it I should have the best opportunity of communion with God, and promoting the salvation of my own soul." From 1725 to 1739 he was the faithful, laborious pastor of the church of Windham, Ct., where he married, in 1727, Mary, the daughter of his predecessor in the ministry, Rev. Samuel Whiting. Of their five children only two daughters reached maturity: one of whom married David Wooster, afterwards major-general in the Revolutionary war; the other married Timothy Pitkin of Farmington, son of the Governor, and father of Timothy Pitkin, the well-known statesman and historian.

In 1739 Mr. Clap was chosen, and in 1740 publicly inducted as President of Yale College. He brought to the office a high reputation for extensive and varied learning—particularly in theology, intellectual and moral philosophy, civil and ecclesiastical law, mathematics and natural science. He made the first orrery ever constructed in America. He was well versed in ancient and modern history. Indeed, from the eulogies of his successors, Presidents Stiles and Dwight, it would seem that there was little worth knowing that he did not know! He had also uncommon executive energy and skill for business affairs, to which Yale owes not a little of her prosperity. He made a new code of college laws—the first book ever printed in New Haven—improved the library and prepared classified catalogues of it, secured a more liberal college charter, increased the number of teachers, raised the standard of scholarship, secured the building of a new college edifice and chapel, and later—in no small degree by his own gift—a house for the theological professor. In pushing these labors, he seems to have had almost unbounded influence with the Legislature. It paid £53 sterling to the church of Windham as a consolation for their loss in parting with him, and afterwards appears to have voted just about as President Clap said was right. And there came a time when this influence did him good service. The President was staunch in defence of what he regarded as sound doctrine and good order in the church, and could not endure what he called "the erratic course" of Whitefield. His outspoken opposition brought him into collision with many of the clergy and other influential men of the State, with whom controversies ensued. The Legislature was invoked (in vain) to put a stop to the President's "arbitrary management" of the college; teachers resigned and were removed; and finally the President, tired of contention, resigned in 1765, and died in 1767, in his 64th year.

Among his more important published works were a History of Yale College, an Introduction to the Study of the Bible, a History and Vindication of the Doctrines of the New-England Churches, and various Treatises, theological, metaphysical and scientific. Many of his valuable manuscripts were burned or lost, in Tryon's predatory expedition against New Haven.

President Stiles accounts for President Clap's massive learning, as the fruit of remarkable industry and method. Pursuing every study on a well-ordered system, "he amassed and digested a valuable treasure of erudition, having prosecuted all the variety of capital subjects in the whole circle of literature. He was indefatigable in his labors, both secular and scientific, for the benefit of the College. For proof we have the college edifice and chapel, and his frequent published dissertations on all kinds of literature." President Dwight says, "There can be little doubt that President Clap was the greatest man who ever sat at the head of this Institution."

Gratefully accepting President Dwight's generous judgment, we are quite ready to believe that greater men have filled that honored seat *since* Mr. Clap's day!

Mr. Richard Woodhull, eminent for learning, who for five years was Tutor under President Clap's administration, and was not personally very friendly to him, says, "In whatever company he was, and whatever the subject of conversation, he appeared evidently to understand it more clearly and comprehensively than any other person present." The most serious defect in the President's character and administration is said to have been, that "he was prone to consider boys as being men"! What does this show, but that he was about a century in advance of his age!

"As to his person," says President Stiles, "he was not tall, yet being thick-set, he appeared rather large and bulky. His aspect was light, placid, serene and contemplative. He was a calm, still, judicious, great man."

The following is the Epitaph inscribed on his grave-stone in New Haven:—

Here lyeth interred the body of the
Reverend and Learned Mr. THOMAS CLAP,
the late president of Yale College, in New Haven.

A truly great man, a gentleman of superior natural genius, most assiduous application, and indefatigable industry. In the various branches of learning he greatly excelled; an accomplished instructor; a patron of the college; a great divine; bold for the truth; a zealous promoter and defender of the doctrines of grace; of unaffected piety, and a pattern of every virtue, the tenderest of fathers and best of friends, the glory of learning, and an ornament of religion; for thirteen years, the faithful and much respected pastor of the church in Windham; and, near 27 years, the laborious and faithful president of the college. And having served his own generation, by the will of God, with serenity and calmness, he fell on sleep, the 7 day of January, 1767 in his 64 year.

Death, great proprietor of all,
'Tis thine to tread out empires
And to quench the stars.

REV. THOMAS, OF SCITUATE.

There was another THOMAS, son of John, a cousin of the President, born in Scituate, 1705, graduated at Harvard, 1725, who seems have been a man of more than ordinary gifts; was pastor in Taunton, 1729–38, when he resigned, returned to Scituate and spent the rest of his life there, serving the church and the town as a layman. He was Colonel of the militia, Justice of the Peace, for many years Representative in the General Court, and a Judge of Plymouth County. He was struck with palsy, while on the bench, and died, 1774, in his 69th year.

REV. NATHANIEL CLAP, OF NEWPORT.

Rev. NATHANIEL, grandson of Nicholas, born at Dorchester, 1669, graduated, Harvard, 1690, began to preach in Newport, 1695, continued, under many discouragements, till 1720, when a church was formed and he was ordained pastor.

He was *another* of the firm defenders of the faith, and after about three years he ceased to administer the ordinances, on the ground that "the members were not of sufficient holy conversation to receive them." Of course there was a storm. The church asked that they might go to other churches for sacramental privileges. But he said, *No.* He had pretty high notions of ministerial authority, and really seems to furnish a single example of *one* of the Clapp race, *rather disposed to have his own way!*

The people grew rebellious, and inclined to have *their* way. And this church having no good *Deacon* Clapp—of whom the family has furnished so many—to manage matters with characteristic gentleness and shrewdness, there came a crisis. The people demanded that their pastor should have a colleague, to preach half the day and administer the ordinances. And two young men in succession did so serve for a short time. But the old gentleman "set down his foot" again, shut his colleague out of the pulpit, and the church split in two. Mr. Clap served the first church until his death, in 1745, aged 77, having preached nearly fifty years.

He was a bachelor, very studious in his habits, so dignified in his bearing that Dean Berkeley, who esteemed him very highly for his good works, said, "Before I saw Father Clap, I thought the Bishop of Rome had the gravest aspect of any man I ever saw; but really the minister of Newport has the most venerable appearance." Whitefield, too, who seems to have been on better terms with Nathaniel than with President Thomas, said that "he was the most venerable man he ever saw"; adding, "He looked like a good old Puritan, and gave me an idea of what stamp those men were who first settled New-England. His countenance was very heavenly, and he prayed most affectionately for a blessing on my coming to Rhode Island. I could not but think I was sitting with one of the patriarchs."

He was undoubtedly a thorough scholar, a pure and saintly man, most generous of time, labor, money, for the good of his people—his usefulness marred only by his stern view of ministerial prerogative and responsibility. And yet he was a man of the kindest heart, of genial humor, a genuine lover of children, for whose welfare he laid himself out in many ingenious devices. You may have seen our annalist's story of the little girl who brought him a present; when he set before her a piece of money, a dish of fruit, and a book, telling her to take her choice. She chose the book; which so pleased him that he gave her the money and the fruit also.

In a commemorative sermon, the Rev. Mr. Callender says of him, "The main stroke in his character was his eminent sanctity and piety, and his desire to promote the knowledge and practice of true godliness in others. He had little value for the form of godliness without its power. He abounded in acts of beneficence to the poor, to whom he was as a kind father and guardian. He remarkably excelled in his care for the education and welfare of children and servants. He abounded in contrivances to do good, by scattering books of piety and virtue, and was at considerable expense, so to awaken the careless, comfort the feeble-minded, succor the tempted, instruct the ignorant, quicken, animate and encourage all. The conclusion of his life and ministry was a peaceful, happy death, without those raptures which some boast of, but with perfect resignation to the will of God, and good hope in Jesus Christ, who was the sum of his doctrine and the end of his conversation."

REV. THEODORE CLAPP, OF NEW ORLEANS.

Rev. THEODORE, son of Thaddeus, of Easthampton, was born in that town, 1792. He was a child of remarkable gifts, a natural orator; entered Yale College as Junior, in 1811; studied from fourteen to sixteen hours a day, living chiefly on bread and water. This of course broke down his physical system, but for a wonder did not subdue his pluck, nor rob him of his good sense. "Afoot and alone" he went out into the wilderness and "vegetated" for seven months, till his strength returned, when he resumed his studies, a wiser and more careful man. He graduated with honor in 1814, intending to study Law, but moved by the sudden death of a beloved classmate, resolved to enter the ministry; studied Theology in Andover, was licensed in 1817; travelled in the South, preached in the hotel of a Kentucky watering-place, where two members of the first Presbyterian church of New Orleans heard and admired him. This led to his settlement, in 1822, as pastor of that church—a no less eloquent successor of the eloquent Sylvester Larned. In New Orleans he soon acquired an unbounded influence.

In 1834 he embraced Unitarian views, and later was understood to have modified these, going still further from the system early studied in Andover, but of which he seems never to have had very clear or consistent ideas. He continued to preach, however, to many of the same hearers, in a building furnished him, free of expense, for twenty-eight years, by Judah Touro, a wealthy Jew, who shared the respect for Mr. Clapp as a Christian citizen that was felt by all alike, whether native or foreign, Protestant, Catholic or Jew: an esteem well earned by thirty-five years of self-forgetting devotion to sufferers of all nations and conditions, through not less than twenty terribly fatal epidemics, including yellow fever and cholera. Summer after summer, when others fled for safety, he remained to personally care for the sick, the dying and the dead; dispensing in gifts to the sufferers more than $40,000 of his own earnings, more than $20,000 furnished by Mr. Touro, and large sums entrusted to him by other benevolent persons in the city.

From all these labors and exposures he rested but once, for a trip to Europe, until his health gave way, and he resigned in 1857; the next year published an interesting volume of Reminiscences of his strange New Orleans experiences, and died, in Louisville, Ky., in May, 1866.

The convictions and sympathies of many of us (certainly my own) are with the doctrines of Mr. Clapp's earlier and not his later ministry. We may not admire the tone in which he sometimes spoke of other beliefs than his own; but surely we can all appreciate and love the personal purity, self-sacrificing humanity and devotion to others' welfare, that were manifest to all who knew him.

The many admirers of his preaching speak of him much in the strain he was himself wont to use of his predecessor, Larned. In form and gesture he was impressive, copious in language and felicitous in illustration. He spoke without full manuscript, from carefully prepared briefs; at once took captive his hearers, and on the wings of his fervid eloquence carried them whithersoever he pleased.—Would that he were here, filling this place to-day, thrilling us with his magnificent periods, fulfilling the purpose of those who for years have meditated this gathering, and realizing his own desire when he wrote, in 1858, "I should be delighted, in company with the descendants of Capt. Roger Clap, to revisit the beautiful spot where repose the ashes of our fathers, where were our early homes, our first warm loves, our first bright hopes —'those pleasant fields traversed so oft in life's morning march, when our bosoms were young.' Though I have been living South for forty-one years, I have lost none of my partiality for Massachusetts, and I can say with Horace that were it possible for me to be born again, and choose my parents, I would not exchange my actual lineage for that of any other person living, however rich, honored, famed or great."

LAWYERS.

But few of our name have studied the profession of Law. One, however, JAMES Clapp, of Oxford, Chenango Co., N. Y., was very eminent as a lawyer, a citizen and a scholar. He began life under great discouragements, but overcame them all. He studied his profession with one of the most eminent jurists in the country—the celebrated Aaron Burr. He argued before juries with great force. His premises were clear, comprehensive and well defined; his deductions, it is said, were like the onward movement of a majestic river, sweeping away every opposing obstacle. He was born in New York, in 1786, and died at his residence in Oxford, Jan. 8, 1854. At a meeting of the Supreme Court and the members of the bar, eloquent and touching tributes were paid to his memory. George A. Starkweather, Esq., referred, among other things, to his being a member of the "Unadilla Hunt," a club formed for hunting deer on the borders of the river of that name:—"In his sports he was governed by the same strict rules of propriety, which governed him in all the acts of his long and useful life. He always gave the game fair play. No noble stag as he snuffed the breeze, with antlers high, driven from his covert to the open field, was ever meanly shot down, as he stopped in his course to survey the danger. The charge was nobly withheld until the buck was on the move. He always gave the bird the flight; the woodcock and plover were not shot in their covert place; he considered it fair notice, that if it could escape the ball of his unerring rifle, it was entitled to its liberty. He was a gentleman of the old school. He was dignified without being haughty, courteous and affable, fond of wit and sharp repartee, participating in the hearty laugh, but never forgetting the gentleman. He was not only a thorough-bred lawyer and gentleman, but he had enriched his mind with all the learning and beauties of the old standard authors, of which Shakspeare was his favorite. He possessed fine colloquial powers, and was the centre of attraction in the social circle. Gov. Daniel S. Dickinson, in his address before the Supreme Court, said of him, "As a member of society he was regarded with respect and veneration, and was sought as a companion for the mature, and a model of imitation by the young, because of his stern unyielding integrity, and the spotless morality of his life. As a lawyer he was profoundly versed in the intricacies of his profession; not in its shifting resorts and devices. He had explored the rich and varied treasures of its learning; its noble and elevating principles, and its best storehouses of accumulated wisdom. He was gifted with captivating conversational powers, and enjoying in a high degree moments of social relaxation. The most intimate friend never ventured to trifle with that personal dignity which attended him on all occasions. He has pleaded his last cause before earthly tribunals. That erect and manly form will repose upon the banks of his beloved Chenango, but the deathless spirit has gone to submit the great issue of life to that Court of *dernier resort*, from whose judgment there is no appeal."

A much younger and only brother of James—JOHN, of Binghamton, N. Y. — is of the same profession. It was in the office of the latter (that of Clark and Clapp) that Hon. Daniel S. Dickinson was a student at law. This brother has retired from the

Bar, and now "rests on his laurels." He entertains and enjoys the most cultivated society in his vicinity, and is surrounded with and appreciates the best literature of the day. Were he not here present, much more might with propriety be said of him.

Ebenezer, a descendant of Thomas, born in Mansfield, Mass., January 21, 1779, graduated at Harvard College in 1799, and settled in Bath, Me. He was a highly respectable man, educated a lawyer, and stood high among his associates and the public. He was one of the Trustees of Bowdoin College, and died in 1856.

TEACHERS.

In this noble profession, not a few of both sexes have shed honor on the family name. Of these one of the most prominent was Noah, born 1718, graduated at Harvard 1735, died 1799. He was a son of Dea. Jonathan, grandson of Nathaniel, and great-grandson of the first Nicholas. He studied theology, and was an acceptable preacher, but ill-health compelled him to turn aside from the pulpit, and he taught the grammar school in Dorchester for nearly twenty years. He was selectman and assessor for more than thirty, and town treasurer for forty-seven years. He knew more of the history of the town than any man in it; had a memory truly marvellous, and his conscientiousness of statement became a proverb. Truth, modesty, sincerity, candor and heavenly charity were his predominant traits.

When some of the town records were burned, with his dwelling, he restored the most important of them, from memory. And such was his fidelity, that no one would dispute a fact or date that was given on Noah Clapp's authority. His son Ebenezer (father of our Historian), was deacon in Dorchester for fifty years. One of his daughters married Hon. Ebenezer Seaver, of Roxbury, for ten years a member of Congress.

Another distinguished teacher was Elisha, graduated at Harvard, 1797; was there Tutor in Greek, 1801–3, and for ten years Principal of Sandwich Academy. Bishop Wainwright was one of his favorite pupils.

After acquiring a competence he returned to Boston, and pursued his favorite studies, mathematics and astronomy. Frequent attacks of disease drove him often to milder climates, and he died of paralysis, in 1830, aged 54. He was an active member of the Massachusetts Historical Society, the American Academy of Science, and other learned bodies. To his research are due many of the items incorporated in the manuscript family history.

His wife, a lady of rare intellect and benevolence, was a daughter of Robert Treat Paine, one of the signers of the Declaration of Independence.

PHYSICIANS.

As a representative of our Physicians who have ceased from their labors, we will name ASAHEL Clapp, son of Reuben, of the stock of Nicholas. He was born in Rutland, Mass., about 1792, but in childhood removed with his parents to Montgomery, in northern Vermont, where he was reared on a backwoods farm, with such educational facilities as the district school afforded.

At about twenty years of age, he came unheralded into the study of Dr. Benjamin Chandler, of St. Albans, saying that he wished to commence at once the study of medicine, and to pay his way by work upon the doctor's farm, or at anything else which he could be set about. The doctor soon recognized the signs of a sharp intellect and shrewd good sense in his roughly-clad pupil, and set him at study with his son. Young Clapp developed a surprising quickness, industry, enthusiasm, and an unconquerable will; soon mastered the doctor's medical works, then devoured whatever he could find upon various branches of natural science—verifying the text by ingenious original experiments, some of which were not only instructive to himself, but useful to others: as when he cured his chum of late rising, by a scientific application to the sleeping victim, from the doctor's electric battery.

In 1817, our young doctor emigrated, and "set up for himself" in New Albany, Ind., where he died in 1863, aged 70. For many years he was not only one of the leading physicians and surgeons, but one of the most honored devotees of science in his adopted State, keeping up his enthusiastic love of botany, geology, microscopic studies, &c., to the end of life. His collection of botanical, geological and other specimens was the largest in the State. He was a man of excellent character, and widely honored for his public spirit and beneficence.

As chairman of an important committee of the National Medical Association, he prepared a report for the Transactions of that body, which is said to be of great permanent value.

WILLIAM Clapp, lately deceased, who was Collector of the port of Burlington, Vt., and held other important offices under the Government, was a younger brother of this Dr. Asahel.

BUSINESS MEN.

The lives of but few of these, not now living, have been published, and I find it difficult to gather authentic facts. One or two names must for this occasion represent this large and respectable company.

Hon. ASA Clapp, of Portland, Me., was a son of Abiel, of Mansfield, Mass., and a descendant of Thomas, of Dedham, eldest son of Thomas, of Scituate. Asa was early left an orphan, and at the age of sixteen went as substitute for a young man drafted for Gen. Sullivan's expedition to drive the British from Rhode Island. At the end of the campaign he sailed from Boston on a privateer; at the close of the Revolutionary war he was captain of a ship; was in Port au Prince when that city was attacked by the negroes, and, with Joseph Peabody, of Salem, aided the citizens.

He established himself as a merchant in Portland, in 1796, trading extensively and profitably, by numerous vessels, with Europe, the East and West Indies, South America, &c. He was active in the separation of Maine from Massachusetts, and was an efficient member of the Convention for forming the Constitution of Maine, in 1819, and was afterwards a Senator in the Maine legislature. He died in Portland, 1848, in his eighty-sixth year, prosecuting his business up to a few moments before his death. He accumulated, used and left a large property, said to be more than a million dollars, and has been supposed to be perhaps the wealthiest man of the name, thus far.

The *Portland Advertiser* gives him credit not only for great business capacity and energy, but for marked liberality, shown in large contributions to public improvements, in his treatment of unfortunate debtors, and of young men having dealings with him. Among other public legacies, he left $8,000 for the relief of female orphans; $4,000 for fuel for poor widows, &c.

His son, Hon. ASA W. H., married a daughter of General Dearborn, of Massachusetts, and has been for some years a Member of Congress.

His daughter, ELIZABETH, married Hon. Levi Woodbury, of New Hampshire, who was Governor of that State, Secretary of the Navy and of the Treasury, Senator in Congress, and Judge of the Supreme Court of the United States.

There is another business man, descended from the same stock, born in 1811, a grandson of Joshua, of Walpole, and a son of Ellis. Of him our Historian wrote, years ago:—"He is a very energetic business man, living in Buffalo, and Editor of the *Buffalo Express*." If he were not in a position to call me to order for violation of my rule to keep silent as to the living, I should say that his name is ALMON M.; and that "the powers that be" in Washington were shrewd enough to discover that he was just the man to do *honestly* that "public printing" which had for years been such a source of leakage to the Treasury, and of corruption to Congress. We may take an honest pride in the fact that he has been able not only to reform that whole vast business, but to clearly *prove* his honesty, against the malignant devices of corrupt men who thought to "break him down" and once more to get possession of their wonted "spoils." All honor to our worthy kinsman, and chairman, who has come out of the furnace heated by the public enemies, as gold comes from the purifying fires!

WHERE THE CLAPPS LIVE.

You ask, Where are the members of the family mostly living? I suppose that in Dorchester, our ancestral seat, there are and ever have been more than in any other one place. They seem to have felt most *at home* there. In the index to the history of that noble old town, I notice one hundred and forty-one references to our name, and in connections not to be ashamed of. They appear to have had a propensity for giving to the town and church (clock, communion-service, pulpit-bibles, and the like).

In seventy-four of the first ninety-one years of the record, there was always one (often two or three) of our name in the chief town offices. Then for twenty years they appear to have mostly given up the reins to others. But I judge they could not be spared, for in 1749, NOAH, nephew of Rev. Nathaniel, of Newport, came into office, and for forty-seven years was assessor, town clerk, selectman, sometimes all at once. For thirty-eight years he was treasurer—and a handy one he must have been to have around; for about the close of the Revolution the record shows that he often paid out of the treasury when there was nothing in it!

After him the family took another rest of seven years, when Samuel came in, and for seven years was first selectman; then for thirty years, 1817–47, there was again from one to three in office. By that time the Clapps seem to have put things into so good a train, that now *common folks* can passably manage the town affairs!

But as for the *Deacon's* office, that is another matter. The churches of Dorchester, and not a few in *this* vicinity, would hardly think it worth while to try to live without one or more Deacon Clapps; and no wonder, considering what the list has been!

Experience with helpful souls in this relation has brought me to love the men who, using well the office of a deacon, purchase to themselves a good degree. My heart goes out with the pastor of Deacon Hopestill, when he says of him, "Deacon Clap was a very gracious man, endowed with a great measure of meekness and patience, studying and practising the things that make for peace." And then he breaks forth into song:—

" Pastors and churches happy be
With ruling elders such as he;
Present, useful; absent, wanted;
Lived desired; died lamented."

In glancing over the Dorchester tax-list of last year, I find forty-nine names, not all taxed for large sums, but most of them encouraging the hope that we shall not be called on for the support of our " poor relations " there.

Of the families of our name now residing in this town and vicinity, I can give only approximate numbers. They are fewer than formerly—perhaps diminishing year by year, as the young men seek business elsewhere, and the daughters give up their names for others. There remain in Northampton about fifteen families, furnishing thirty-one voters and thirty-seven tax-payers; in Southampton, about twenty voters; in Easthampton perhaps eighteen voters, of whom fifteen are heads of families, and of descendants of the Clapp family, of all names, one hundred and fifteen to one hundred and twenty. Westhampton now has but two families bearing the name, though there are twenty families there tracing back their lineage directly to Elder Preserved. Montague reports twenty families.

But while so many have lived and died in and about Dorchester and Northampton, especially in earlier years, there have within the last century been wanderers enough to indicate our membership in " the universal Yankee nation." There is not a State in New England or the West but has our representatives; and they are found, though fewer of late years, in the South. Among the places of deaths named in the annals, besides all the Northern and older Western States, are Pensacolo, Charleston, Columbia, the island of Jamaica, Sandwich Islands, Rio Janeiro and Rio Grande, and a large number at sea.

While preparing this address, I have been interested to look into such recent (not always the latest) city " Directories " as I could find, for the present abodes of our most active business men. That of Boston (now including Dorchester) gives 124; Charlestown, 8; Chelsea, 7; Cambridge and Lynn, 5 each; Salem, 4; Lowell and Taunton, 2 each; Pittsfield, 8; Newton, Concord, Nashua, Manchester, 1 each; Providence, 10; Pawtucket, 5; Hartford, 14; Norwich, 3; New Haven and Bridgeport, 1 each; Portland, 7; Bath and Augusta, 2 each; Gardiner, St. John and Woodstock, N. B., 1 each; New York and Brooklyn, 30—and not an Alderman, Common Councilman or liquor-dealer among them! Jersey City, Newark, Troy, Buffalo and Saratoga, 4 each; Albany, 7; Auburn, 6; Newburg and White Plains, 3 each; Tarrytown, 2; and we are represented in Oswego, Syracuse, Potsdam, Peekskill, Binghamton, Sing Sing (not in the State-prison). Philadelphia now gives but one name—but the directory sets him down as a "gentleman"; Pittsburg, 3; Baltimore, 1 (and one "Clapsadole"); Washington and Georgetown, 4; Richmond, 1; St. Louis, 2; Louisville, 3; Memphis, 2 (lawyers); New Orleans, 3; Houston, Texas, 2; Sabine, 1; Cincinnati, 4; Detroit, 4; Milwaukee, 1; Chicago, 11; St. Joseph, 1 (city engineer); Leavenworth, 2; Omaha, 1; San Francisco, 6; Sonora, 2; and one or two each in more towns than can be named in every State from Maine to Oregon.

COLLEGE GRADUATES.

Not having had access to all the catalogues, I cannot say how many of our name have received a college education. Sixteen have graduated at Harvard, eight of whom were Dorchester boys. Of these, six became ministers, two physicians, and two teachers. Six have graduated at Yale, of whom three became ministers. Two are now members of Yale. Three have graduated at Brown University; and four at Dartmonth. Eight have studied theology in the Seminary at Andover.

THEIR OCCUPATION.

The occupations of the family have been as various as possible. In the professions we have had ministers, judges, lawyers, physicians, many teachers, and several editors. I am sorry to think that the ministry attracts fewer of our kindred than formerly. Several of the profession have lately died—among them Rev. Dexter, of Salem, and Rev. Sumner G., formerly of St. Johnsbury, Vt.; and as now living I know of but four Congregationalists, three Baptists, three Methodists, one Presbyterian, and one Episcopalian. Among the sons of Clapp mothers, we have several, of whom Rev. Dr. George Putnam, of Roxbury (descended from Deacon Edward), and Rev. Dr. W. H. Furness, of Philadelphia (descended from Capt. Roger, through Rev. Supply), are very widely known.

We have had many cashiers and treasurers. Their neighbors seem not to have feared to trust them with money.

There is scarcely an honest trade unrepresented—from makers of jewelry, watches and philosophical instruments, to the great ship-builders of Bath. Many, especially of the western Massachusetts families, have been farmers; not a few carpenters, tanners, gardeners—not forgetting Thaddeus, our pomologist (graduated Harvard, 1834), producer of the delicious pear, "Clapp's favorite;" manufacturers, merchants, dealers in every honest product. Some, like Jason, of Pittsfield, it seems were able to manage manufacturing, carriage-building, staging, mail-contracting, and so on, and then to have found leisure for legislative and other public services.

Book making and selling has been the favorite business of one branch of the family, including printers, lithographers, &c. Elisha B.'s marriage with a sister of the Hon. Nathan Hale, of the *Boston Daily Advertiser*, perhaps turned the course of some in that direction, as did the family interest of others in Clapp's *Evening Gazette*.

And here let me pay a sacred debt of personal gratitude to that veteran printer and editor, who would have so loved to see this gathering—William Warland Clapp, of the Boston *Evening Gazette*. His kindly notice (and that of his sons) of certain boyish productions, and his frequent words of cheer, roused in me the desire for an education, and the hope of a life not wholly useless to others. To me that benign, fatherly face comes tenderly among the dear memories of to-day.

We have had our full share of State and National Legislators, post-masters, sheriffs, collectors of customs; and our Otis, Assessor of Internal Revenue in *Bòston*—where they don't put unworthy men in office! There was Col. Daniel, member of the provincial Congress, 1774, who for more than thirty years was Register of Deeds in Worcester County. What is best of all, these men left the public service with a good name. And do not flatter yourselves a good name is *cheaply* gained on our Cousin Eben's impartial record. Though he says he has heard of but one as ever arrested for crime, I have read on those pages written only for his own eye, here and there certain descriptive phrases that—we'll not repeat outside of the family!

Military life has proved attractive, and there is scarcely a military title but what has been worn by some member of the family. On the day of the battle of Lexington, five of our name enlisted in one company in Dorchester; seven from that town served through the Revolutionary war; eleven there joined Lieut. Clapp's company for reënforcing the army in 1780, and five Dorchester Clapps enlisted for the suppression of Shay's rebellion. In the French and Revolutionary wars, and in that of 1812, the Dorchester and Northampton branches of the family were fully represented, and several lost their lives. I need not say that many hearts with us to-day ache for those out of their homes, who lately fell in defence of our imperilled Union.

THEIR LONGEVITY, ETC.

The Clapps have been a *long-lived* race. Our Historian writes of very many who died in infancy; but there are also many who lived to an extreme age—from 80 to 90 years and upwards. Earl Clapp, of Rochester, died at 98; my own grandfather, Charles, of Northampton, died at 91, my grandmother at 97. Some here remember the patriarch, Benjamin, of Easthampton, who at the age of 92 was a constant attendant at church. His wife died in 1847, over 97 years old, the mother of fifteen children, thirteen of whom lived to be heads of families, so that she lived to see 70 grandchildren, and as many great-grandchildren. Rachel, daughter of Benjamin Clapp, of East-hampton, and wife of Nathaniel Edwards, of Northampton, lived to the age of 100 years, 4 months and 11 days.

That this has been a *fruitful* vine, is self-evident, without taking account of the many families that number from ten to fifteen children, and more; or citing at least one case of triplets, and another, of two pairs of twins presented to one father in fifty-one weeks.

Frequent notices in the annals not only prove our historian's faith that the Clapps have been famed for a genuine old-time courtesy—the politeness of a truly kind heart—but also his persuasion that ours is a *good-looking* family! I should not dare to read aloud his notes set against the names of some of you, who have somehow got upon his susceptible side. But that with all this there goes generally a solid *good sense*, he quietly assumes.

And yet there does appear to have been, many years ago, *one* Clapp (I never heard of another), who was something of a *dandy* in his way. He was one Robert, Captain of a vessel sailing from Boston to the West Indies. In the inventory of his property, in his will, we find "one light blue broadcloth coat and breeches, and one dark blue ditto, trimmed with silver"; "one pair velvet breeches"; "black padusoy jacket, with gold buttons"; "one-eighth of brig Seahorse," and "one negro man, worth £100"!

He was from England, his wife lived there; and he seems scarcely to have made this country his home. With him and his negro man, worth £100, the glory of velvet breeches, silver trimmings and gold buttoned jackets departed from the family forever! Alas, for our one vanished dandy!

HISTORICAL MATERIAL.

These statistics seem dry enough; but do not judge from this that the family annals have not in them elements of romantic and often of deeply affecting interest. We may find them in the story of Lewis and Enos (sons of Nathaniel, of Dorchester), whose was a love like David and Jonathan's, leading them to live together unmarried till past forty years of age. So seldom were they separate, that when the children saw either they cried out, all the same, "There goes Lewis and Enos!" We find them in the story of Captains Caleb and Joshua (sons of Joel, of Sudbury), so alike that few could distinguish them; both of them Captains in the Revolution, and friends of Gen. Washington; both represented their towns in the Legislature; both remarkably winning, but subject to fits of despondency which led to their deaths by suicide. We find them in the story of Edward, of Milton, lost in the expedition to Canada against the Indians, 1690; in that of John, of Sudbury, who died in the Crown Point expedition; that of Joseph, of Deerfield, through whose hat the Indians put three bullets; that of Mrs. Sarah, of Deerfield, whom the Indians carried into captivity; that of Dr. Eleazer, a graduate of Harvard, who in a fit of derangement took his own life, and was in five days followed by his mother, ending hers in the same way; that of the young husband killed by accident in thirteen days after his marriage; in the story of those who left home for other shores, and were heard of no more; in the several instances in which husband and wife, brother and sister, parent and child, have died so near each other as to be buried in the same grave; in the noble self-sacrifice of the widow Ann S. Merrick, of Springfield, daughter of Cephas Clapp, who with the 10th Mass. Volunteers went into the late army of the Union, and whose tender care of the sick and wounded attracted the admiring notice of President Lincoln; in the sad fate of the promising Boston medal scholar, who died in Boston harbor, almost in sight of his father's door, on his return from an East India voyage in pursuit of health; and in the still sadder death of Edward and John, hopeful sons of Deacon John, of Roxbury, who were drowned together while on a pleasure excursion—all of the family, parents, brother and sisters, being near by.

Yes; in those two seemingly frigid volumes of statistics, are the elements of many a thrilling story, that would move us alternately to laughter and to tears.

But those stories must be left for the lips and pens of others. It was long ago time to relieve your patience. Enough for me, if these crude statements shall have moved your gratitude to God, and quickened your interest to know more of his dealings with a family, so numerous, so widely scattered, so richly blessed. The materials for such knowledge are now extant, and the Historian still lives who has gathered, and can fitly set them forth—not only for *our* profit, but as a precious contribution to the history of the past and passing generations.

Various as have been the characters, circumstances and fortunes of the family, we must be blind indeed, not to recognize the honor God has put upon it, in the marked *Piety* which so distinguished our ancestors, as a body, and has been the blessed inheritance of so many of their descendants.

Who of us cannot truthfully and feelingly say with Cowper:

> " My boast is not that I deduce my birth
> From loins enthroned, and rulers of the earth ;
> But higher yet my proud pretensions rise—
> The child of parents passed into the skies ! "

Amid the joys of such an inheritance, let us recognize its responsibilities. Let us accept and take up the duties which, as descendants of those great-hearted, godly Pilgrim Fathers, we owe to an age so different from theirs ; to a government they had so large a share in founding ; to principles and institutions they prized so highly ; to a land for which they sacrificed so much and prayed so fervently.

That august and goodly company ! we can almost see them hovering over us to-day, with many of their lineage—our nearer kindred — a great cloud of witnesses compassing us about ; here and there a gray-haired Patriarch, bearing on his aged heart some little lamb that but yesterday was the light of our homes : —thus linking the generations, and thrilling our hearts with the pulsations of that tie of kindred, which of the living and the dead but one communion makes.

We may lack the genius, the culture, the enthusiasm, of some of our honored kindred; and may fancy that we lack their call and their opportunity to move the world upward, and to leave on it the print of our uplifting hands.

But who can say what opportunities Providence may make for us, if we, prepared, are waiting and watching for them? Suddenly, as on the trite, level life of this land, nine years ago, God sprung the issues of the great Rebellion, that made heroes of the obscurest, so He may at any hour call *us* into crises that shall demand a valor, self-denial, energy and faith, not less than those which our fathers opposed to the tyranny of Elizabeth and James and the Charleses of the old country, and the oppressors of the colonists in the new.

But no one of us need sigh for greater talents, nor wait for grander opportunities. Not on thrones alone are souls made kingly; not on battle-fields alone are victories won and lost. Our humblest homes may be made abodes of saintliest royalty; in the dustiest paths of our work-day life, we are daily gaining or losing heaven. Each has his gifts, his place, his work appointed of God—a work worthy of the worthiest—and for that work, well done or ill, each is to give account.

When we go from this pleasant gathering, shall we not part with the mutual pledge to do our utmost, each in his several sphere, to maintain the principles our fathers loved even unto death, to build up the kingdom of our fathers' God—that God who setteth the solitary in families—that Redeemer in whom all the families of the earth are blessed!

PROCEEDINGS, READING OF PAPERS, &c.

AFTER the delivery of the Address, which was listened to, throughout, with the most marked attention, and several portions of which drew forth the applause of the audience, the well-known and favorite song of "America" was sung, the assembly rising and joining in this delightful part of the exercises of the day.

The President then introduced to the meeting, OTIS CLAPP, Esq., of Boston, who read the following paper:—

THE PURITAN BROTHERHOOD; ITS ORIGIN AND OBJECTS; AND THE CONNECTION OF THE CLAPP FAMILY THEREWITH.

The early members of our family were moved to emigrate to this country, because of their sympathy in the Puritan brotherhood. That brotherhood was a child of the Reformation.

The struggle, out of which came Puritanism, and its principles, was among the most memorable, in its character and results, in the world's history. It is common to measure events by centuries. In this connection, the fact is a striking one, that Pope Leo's bull, excommunicating Martin Luther, was in the year 1520; and the departure of the May Flower from the shores of Europe, with its freight of Pilgrims, was in 1620—just one century after.

It seems, in the providence of God, as though that century was given over to what was called King-craft, and Priest-craft, and allowed full sway for experiments in human dominion, persecution, and all methods, but Divine methods, to *force unity in civil and religious affairs.*

Out of this fiery furnace came the Puritans, or those who believed that churches and commonwealths should be based upon the Word of God, and imbued with His Spirit. Hume divides them into three classes, viz.:—"Political Puritans," "Doctrinal Puritans," and "Puritans in Discipline." The strict meaning of the term was, "One who is scrupulous and strict in his religious life." Such teachers are now recognized and tolerated as a matter of course. But up to the time of the Commonwealth in 1648, they were imprisoned, banished, executed, and persecuted in all conceivable ways.

From the period when Henry VIII. ascended the throne of England, in 1509, to the Commonwealth in 1648—139 years—England had six Sovereigns, viz.: Henry VIII., 1509 to 1546, reigned 37 years; Edward VI., 1547 to 1553, reigned 6 years; Mary, 1553 to 1558, reigned 5 years; Elizabeth, 1558 to 1602, reigned 44 years; James I., 1603 to 1624, reigned 21 years; Charles I., 1625 to 1648, reigned 23 years. A glance at these Sovereigns may help to give an idea of the school in which the Puritans were trained. Catholicism was introduced into England, as the established religion, by William the Conqueror, about 1067.

HENRY VIII. started as a good Catholic. He wrote a reply to Luther, for which the Pope gave him the title of "Defender of the Faith." He married Catherine of Aragon, daughter of Ferdinand and Isabella—lived with her 18 years, and then put her away. He asked the Pope for a divorce, which was declined. Whereupon he turned Protestant. In short, he made himself *head* of the church, instead of a *subordinate* to the Pope. He then married five wives in ten years, viz.:—Anna Boleyn, in 1533; Jane Seymour, in 1536; Anna of Cleves, in 1540; Catherine Howard, also in 1540; Catherine Parr, in 1543.

Some idea of Henry VIII. may be gained from the following extracts from one of his Statutes:—

"There shall be no annotations or preambles in Bibles or New Testaments *in English*. The Bible shall not be read *in English* in any church.

"No women, or artificers, apprentices, journeymen, serving-men, husbandmen, or laborers, shall read the New Testament *in English*.

"Nothing shall be taught or maintained contrary to the King's instructions.

"If any spiritual person shall be convict of preaching, or maintaining anything contrary to the King's instructions already made, or hereafter to be made, he shall for the first offence recant; for the second, bear a fagot; and for the third, be burnt."—*Stat.* 35 Henry VIII.

Now this was the law of a professedly Protestant King, and adhered to by the succeeding monarchs, in letter and spirit, for more than ninety years, embracing the reigns of *Mary*, *Elizabeth*, *James I.* and *Charles I.*

The act of Henry VIII. was a bold one; "but as for any amendment of the doctrines of popery," says Neale, "any further than was necessary to secure his own supremacy," and "the revenues of the church," "he had not the honor to accomplish."

EDWARD VI. ascended the throne at nine years of age, and died at the age of fifteen. He was provided with sixteen Regents to manage affairs—ten for the Reformation, and six for the old religion. During this brief reign, the rigors of the last began to be relaxed; persecution was stopped, and prison doors were set open. The Reformation made quick progress. The controversy that gave rise to separation now began. The "occasion was, that Bishop Hooper refused to be consecrated in the popish habits;" as "the administrations of priests were *thought to receive their validity from the consecrated vestments.*"

Mary occupied the throne from 1553 to 1558, five years. She made use of her power to turn things back into the old channel. Popery revived, and a second time became the established religion of the Church of England. The Statutes of King Edward were repealed, and the penal laws against heretics were put in execution against Reformers. Many were imprisoned, scourged, executed. Great numbers fled to Germany, Switzerland, and Geneva. Neale says her reign "ought to be transmitted in characters of blood." Some three hundred persons suffered at the stake as heretics, in less than four years.

Queen Elizabeth's accession to the crown gave new life to the Reformation. The Pope had pronounced her illegitimate, which helped to give her a bias towards the Protestants, whom she protected in some degree. She was regarded as a politic princess, and the glory of the age. Yet she had high notions of the *sovereign authority* of princes, and of *absolute supremacy* in church affairs. Although disliking the *authority* of Rome, she liked its forms and ceremonies. She disliked the Puritans, and resorted to extreme severity to enforce these forms and ceremonies upon them. To this, their consciences objected; because these were, to them, the symbols of popery—of Satan—and not authorized by Scripture, their *only* authority.

Elizabeth looked upon all such objections with no favor. She countenanced all the engines of persecution, such as "Spiritual Courts," "High Commissions," "Star Chamber," &c.—whose trials and persecutions would almost rival the Spanish Inquisition. The prisons were filled with many of the most pure and quiet men in the kingdom, for non-conformity to these forms and ceremonies.

Two attempts were made in Parliament to reach these Courts; and Attorney Morris offered a bill to prohibit "illegal imprisonments." As soon as Queen Elizabeth heard of this, "she sent for Speaker Coke, and commanded him to tell the House that it was wholly in *her power* to call, to determine, to assent, or dissent, to *anything* done in Parliament; that it was not meant that they should meddle with matters of State, or causes ecclesiastical; that she wondered they should attempt a thing so contrary to her commandment; that she was highly offended at it," &c. &c. Mr. Morris, who offered the bill, was "seized by a Sergeant-at-arms, discharged from office, disabled from practice, and kept for some years a prisoner."

And yet, in the face of all such efforts, the Puritans continued to increase, and began to obtain a majority in the House of Commons, even in Elizabeth's reign.

The term *Puritan* was given as a name of reproach to those who "refused to subscribe to the liturgy, ceremonies, and discipline of the church." "The controversy with the Puritans," says Neale, "had only a small beginning, viz., the imposing of the popish habits, and a few indifferent ceremonies; but it opened by degrees into a reformation of discipline, which all confessed was wanting; and at last the doctrinal articles were debated. The queen and the later bishops would not part with a *pin* out of the hierarchy, nor leave a latitude in the most trifling ceremonies, but insisted upon an exact uniformity both in doctrine and ceremonies."

"The Puritans," he continues, "were the most resolved Protestants in the nation. They were in all ranks, but generally from the mercantile and middling classes. Their behavior was severe and rigid, far removed from the fashionable freedoms and vices of the age." "With all their faults, they were the most pious and devout people in the land; *men of prayer*, both in secret and in public, as well as in their families." "They were circumspect as to all excesses of eating, drinking, apparel, and lawful diversions; being frugal in house-keeping, industrious in their particular callings, honest and exact in their dealings, and solicitous to give every one his own." (Vol. i. 399.)

These are the qualities required to make good Christians and good citizens. Elizabeth and her adherents overlooked these qualities, and allowed them to receive "cruel mockings, bonds, and imprisonments."

JAMES I.—The Pilgrims left England for this country during this reign. James was an indolent and vain-glorious monarch, a willing captive to his bishops, who flattered his vanity, and put into his head the maxim, "No bishop, no king." "No prince was ever so much flattered, who so little deserved it." Here is one of his "directions," or laws, which will serve as a sample of his statesmanship. "That no preacher of any degree soever, shall henceforth presume in auditory to declare, limit, or set bounds to the prerogative, power, or jurisdiction of Sovereign princes, or meddle with affairs of State." "He was," according to Bishop Burnet, "the scorn of the age; a mere pedant, without true judgment, courage, or steadiness; his reign being a continued course of mean practices." "He was certainly the meanest prince that ever sat upon the British throne."

CHARLES I. came to the throne in 1625. He dissolved the parliament, dispensed with the lords and commons, and directed affairs by authority of king and council. No one could speak or write against these proceedings without the utmost hazard of his liberty and estate. The church was governed by like arbitrary and illegal methods. Dr. Laud, Bishop of London, was prime minister, "and pursued his wild scheme of uniting the two churches of England and Rome without the least regard to the rights of conscience, or laws of the land, bearing down opposition with unrelenting severity. To make way for this union, the churches were not only to be repaired, but ornamented with pictures, paintings, images, altar-pieces, &c.; the forms of public worship were to be decorated with a number of pompous rites and ceremonies, in imitation of the church of Rome; and the Puritans, who were the professed enemies of everything that looked like popery, were to be suppressed, or driven out of the land." "To accomplish this, due instructions were issued, which brought a great deal of business into the Spiritual Courts."—*Neale*, Vol. i. 542.

The Puritan ministers were thus "suspended, or deprived, and their families driven to distress. Nor was there any prospect of relief."

I will give one sample of cruelty inflicted upon Dr. Alexander Leighton in 1630, the year in which Dorchester was first settled. He wrote an appeal, calling the bishops "Men of blood." He claimed "that the church has her laws from Scripture, and that no king may make laws for the house of God." The Star Chamber found him guilty. The execution of his sentence was, in the language of Archbishop Laud, Prime Minister of Charles I., as follows:

1. "He was severely whipt before he was put in the pillory."
2. "He had one of his ears cut off."
3. "One side of his nose slit."
4. "Branded on the cheek with a red-hot iron with the letters S. S."

(Sower of Sedition). Seven days after, "the scars upon his back, ear, nose and face, being not yet cured, he was again whipt at the pillory;" and "the remainder of his sentence executed upon him, by cutting off the other ear, slitting the other side of his nose, and branding the other cheek." Then he was thrown into prison, where he continued in close confinement ten years, till he was released by the Long Parliament.

The clouds every day grew thicker, threatening a violent storm, and giving rise to a second grand colony, called Massachusetts-Bay. In the succeeding twelve years of Bishop Laud's administration, there came over to this country some 4000 planters, bringing over in money and goods some £500,000. In this way four settlements were made, viz., Plymouth, Massachusetts-Bay, Connecticut and New Haven. In this way, also, our early towns were settled—Northampton, Hadley, Hatfield and others among them. The leaders into these parts were Puritan ministers, who had been hunted from place to place, until they chose this wilderness as a retreat.

"I have," says Neale, "a list of seventy-seven divines who became pastors of sundry little churches and congregations in that country before the year 1640." "They were not all of the first rank for deep and extensive learning; yet they had a better share of it than most of the neighboring clergy; and, which is of more consequence, they were men of strict sobriety and virtue; plain, serious, affectionate preachers."

Macaulay says of them, "They had been oppressed, and oppression had made them a pure body." Hume, the historian, says it is to the despised sect of Puritans, that we are indebted for the whole freedom in the British Constitution. Dr. Priestley responds, we accept the compliment, but despise the reflection. "No great truth," says Wm. Law, "ever came into the world which was not opposed by the ruling opinions of the time." Through agencies like these, was the brain of New England educated into ideas, which have made themselves felt for good, not only within her own borders, but throughout the world.

Such, in brief, were the main causes which led to the first settlement of Massachusetts. The May Flower arrived at Plymouth in 1620. A fleet, with Mr. Higginson and others, arrived in Salem June 20, 1629. And the "great ship" Mary & John, with our ancestor Roger Clap and others, arrived May 30, 1630. If we recognize God in history, we can hardly fail to see that these men and women were led to struggle with all the evils of bad government, to prepare them to come to a new continent, and establish new institutions, based on the principles of Divine Justice. It is interesting to follow these providential leadings.

"This high abuse of church power," says Neale, "obliged many learned ministers and their followers to leave the kingdom, and retire to Amsterdam, Rotterdam, the Hague, Leyden, Utrecht, &c., in Holland." This movement began in 1604, and John Robinson was one of the leaders. They *there* learned from the Dutch, the system of small townships, of small republics, and of small commonwealths. These they planted *here*, where they found a congenial soil. Each town was a commonwealth; and an aggregation of towns, was an enlarged commonwealth, or republic. The intelligent and faithful performance of town duties is one of the grand agencies of our civilization.

In this field of duty, our family ancestors have had an active and an honorable share. In the first one hundred years from the formation of the government of Massachusetts—say from 1629 to 1729—members of the Clapp family held seats in the Legislature sixty-two years. Roger and his three sons, viz., Samuel, Hopestill, and Preserved, held seats in the Legislature forty-four years. The town of Scituate was represented by Thomas, Samuel, Nathaniel, and Stephen Clapp, sixteen years, between 1680 and 1710. These men are represented as honest, earnest, outspoken, God-fearing men.

The intelligent and faithful performance of these Town, State and Church duties, may appear to some as matters of minor consideration; but such is not the estimate of that clear-headed political economist and statesman, DeTocqueville. "On the continent of Europe," he says, "at the beginning of the seventeenth century, absolute monarchy had everywhere triumphed over the ruins of the oligarchical and feudal liberties of the Middle Ages. Never perhaps were the ideas of right more completely overlooked, than in the midst of the splendor of Europe; never was there less activity among the people; never were the principles of true freedom less widely circulated; and at that very time, those principles, which were scorned or unknown by the nations of Europe, were proclaimed in the deserts of the new world, and were accepted as the future creed of a great people. The boldest theories of the human mind were reduced to practice by a community so humble, that not a statesman condescended to attend to it."

"In New England," he says, "townships were completely and definitely constituted as early as 1650." "The independence of the township was the nucleus round which the local interests, passions, rights, and duties, collected and clung. It gave scope to the activity of a real political life, thoroughly democratic and republican."

Again, "municipal institutions constitute the strength of free nations. Town-meetings are to liberty, what primary schools are to science—they bring it within the people's reach."

The movement which led the Puritans to plant churches, and civil institutions, based upon the simple principles of the Divine Word, I understand to be as much the work of the Divine Providence, as was the leading of the Israelites *out of bondage, through the Red Sea and through the wilderness*, into the promised land. They, too, were led "by a pillar of cloud by day," and "a pillar of fire by night," *visible* to all His true worshippers. When there was a plague of *thick darkness* in all the land of Egypt three days, "all the children of Israel had *light in their dwellings*." All may have this light, who comply with the requisite conditions. This promised land did not consist of broad acres of beautiful forests, pastures and meadows merely, but in those spiritual and celestial graces which they so well typify, and which are all comprehended in obedience to the command, on which hang the Law and the Prophets. We often hear the remark, "Yes, the Puritans were persecuted. But when they got the power, they did the same thing." Such persons would do well to read and inwardly digest the facts of history—and base their opinions thereon. They had sufficient sagacity and good sense, after coming to this wilderness to set up religious and civil institutions, new to the society in which they had lived, not to risk their destruction, by either opposition or indifference. They had inherited legacies of intolerance and its fruits, as has been shown. In some cases they allowed themselves, more naturally than properly, to indulge in similar mistakes. But these cases were exceptional and occasional.

Roger Clap came to Dorchester in 1630. "I found it," he says, "a vacant wilderness in respect of English. There were some English at Plymouth and Salem, and some few at Charlestown, who were very destitute when we came ashore." Dorchester first chose town officers in 1633. It is claimed that Dorchester was the first town that ever chose Selectmen, either in this country or any other. Roger was chosen one of the Selectmen in 1637. He was then about twenty-seven years of age, and was an active public man for over fifty years thereafter. He served the town as Selectman seventeen years; and as Representative to the General Court. sixteen years. In 1637 the whole General Court, including Governor, Lieut. Governor, Senators, and Representatives, consisted of only thirty-five persons.

In 1634 there was levied a tax of £600 for public uses, on twelve plantations. Nearly one half was assessed upon Dorchester, New-Town and Boston, in sums of £80 each. The corporate existence of Dorchester commenced four years before, in 1630, and ended with 1869, having had an honorable duration of two hundred and thirty-nine years.

Five Clapps came to Dorchester, viz.: Roger, in 1630; Edward, Nicholas and Thomas, in 1633; and John subsequently. John died without issue. Thomas settled in Scituate. All of this name, so far as is known, are descended from Roger, Edward, Nicholas and Thomas. They were strong Puritans, and entered with heart and soul into the work of founding churches, towns and other civil institutions. Liberty, with hunger, was sweet, compared with plenty without it. "Bread was so very scarce," says Roger, "that the very crusts of my father's table would have been sweet unto me." Notwithstanding these privations, he thanked God for contentedness in these straits, "and advised his dear brethren," Edward, Nicholas, Thomas, and his two sisters, to come also. They took his advice, "sold their means, and came hither."

The Clapps seemed to take to State, Town and Church affairs, as naturally as a bird to the air. In the matter of offices, where there was a large amount of work required, with no compensation—except in the consciousness of doing good—the Clapps always occupied an advanced position. So in the military line. If a corporal, sergeant, ensign, lieutenant, or captain, was wanted for the militia—which was an institution of vast importance in those days—they were too modest to decline the honor; and doubtless showed a becoming gratitude, performing well the duty, and acknowledging the compliment by giving the accustomed "entertainment."

A few facts will illustrate this position. In Dorchester, members of the Clapp family have served as—Selectmen, 133 years; Representatives in the General Court, 41 years; Town Treasurer, 44 years; Assessors, 46 years; Town Clerk, 52 years. Here is an aggregate of 316 years. But this does not include many others, such as Overseer of the Poor, first filled by Nicholas; School Committee, Constable, and many other offices. If a church was to be built, its broken glass set—here, too, Nicholas is on record as the first committee-man—or otherwise repaired; if the people had to be seated in church by a committee; if an ordination or a neighboring church council was held, requiring a committee or delegates, *they* were expected to help fill the places of honor.

There was much of the same in Scituate.

The first Church in Dorchester was organized on the other side of the water, and came over in a body with its ministers, Messrs. Warham and Maverick. Edward Clapp was Deacon from 1638 to 1664, 26 years. Samuel Clapp, son of Roger, was Deacon and then Ruling Elder, from 1701 to 1708. Hopestill Clapp, son of Roger, was Deacon from 1692 to 1709, and Ruling Elder from 1709 to 1719. Jonathan Clapp, Deacon from 1719 to 1723. Hopestill Clapp, jr., Deacon from 1723 to 1759. Ebenezer Clapp, Deacon from 1809 to 1860. Ebenezer Clapp, jr., Deacon from 1858 to date.

Nicholas Clapp was called Deacon in some of the early records.

Here are eight persons in number, with 177 years of service out of 239.

In looking over the Records of the Massachusetts General Court, I find the first reference to Roger to be in connection with experiments in making saltpetre, in 1642. The record runs thus:—

"And being willing to lay hold on and use all such means as God shall direct us unto, as may tend to the raising and producing such materials amongst ourselves as may perfect the making of gunpowder, the instrumental means all nations lay hold on for their preservations;" "do order and decree that every plantation shall erect an house about 20 or 30 feet long, by 20 foot wide," &c.

Committees were appointed in 21 towns to superintend these experiments. "Sergeant Clap" was appointed for Dorchester.

May 6, 1646, "It is ordered that Humphrey Atherton be Captain of Dorchester Company, Roger Clap Lieftenant, and Hopestill Foster Ensign."

In 1653 Roger was one of a Committee of four to settle differences between Dedham and several Indians.

In 1655, one of a "Committee of two, on a bill of costs," "to return their thoughts to this Court."

Also, Committee of Trade, "whereby merchandizing may be encouraged, and the hands also of the husbandman may not weary in his employment, and for begetting a right understanding, and a loving compliance between both, they may advise together, or assuage as they see cause."

1658, Committee "to lay out a highway thro' Roxbury."

1658, Committee on the petition of the celebrated John Eliot, "to lay out convenient bounds to Natic."

1659, Committee "on petition of Concord about bridges."

1660, Committee "to run South line 40 miles S. W. of Hudson's River." Also, "to encourage settlement of Braintree."

1663, "On the Militia, for rectifying what is amiss, and the better settling of the same." Also, Committee on the Castle.

1664, May 29, Committee on South line betwixt Massachusetts and Plymouth. Oct. 19, "The Court granted it meete to grant Roger Clap fower pounds for his service in laying out the Southern line of our patent between Plymouth and Massachusetts."

1665, Committee on "complaints about tanning leather."

1661, Dec. 31, "Left. Roger Clap, being chosen by the town of Dorchester to end small causes, the Court allows thereof; and at the request of the towne of Dorchester, to appoint one to joyne persons in marriage, that are published according to lawe, the Court doth hereby authorize Left. Roger Clap for the service." He married large numbers.

Aug. 1, 1665. "This Court having considered of the want of a Captain for the Castle, do nominate and appoint Capt. Roger Clap to be Captain thereof."

The Castle was regarded by the colony as a position of great importance. It used to be visited by the Governor and Legislature in a body, and by committees; and provision was made that it should always be in a state of efficiency. From 1633 to 1685—52 years—there were one hundred and twenty-five distinct entries in relation to it on the State Records.

These records say:— "For the better improvement of the Castle for the service of the Country, in times of peace and war, it is ordered by this Court, and the authority thereof, that there shall be a constant settled garrison, consisting of a captain, lieut., and other officers, with 64 able men completely armed—out of trained bands—from Boston 30, Dorchester 12, Charlestown 12, and Roxbury 10." "It being a matter encumbent on this Court to provide that all meete provision be made for the upholding of the Castle, and suitable artillery and batteryes there provided, it is ordered, that the Gov. and Major Generall, for the time being, doe from time to time make such supplies of men and ammunition as the season of the year or the condition and occasion of the country may require."—Vol. iv. Pt. 2, p. 280.

In 1673 the Castle was burned, and "Gov. Leverett, Capt. Clap," and three others, "were a Committee to see what should be done."

The questions and duties which came before Capt. Clap for action, were those which required intelligence, sound judgment and integrity, to dispose of correctly. I never learned that he failed in duty but once. On one occasion a ship passed the Castle without stopping. For this he was fined £50 by the County Court. He asked the General Court to remit the fine. "It appearing," as the records of the Court state, "that his omission of what he ought to have done, proceeded not from any wilful neglect, but from a dubiousness that was upon him by reason of a former order, and the sudden passing of the ship, whereby he was surprised, judge meete to remit his fine." Perhaps this was permitted to show his posterity that he was human; and therefore it would be unadvisable to worship him as a saint!

Thomas Clapp, cousin of Roger, moved to Scituate about 1642. In Deane's History of Scituate, ten gentlemen are spoken of, one of whom was Thomas Clapp, "as men eminently qualified for transacting not only the municipal concerns of the settlement, but for taking part in the government of the colony.". "The next generation suffered in the means of education, and the third generation still more."

The descendants of Thomas Clapp were numerous, and embrace some of the most distinguished men of this name. Deane speaks of a grist mill and fulling mill which belonged to Captain John Clapp in 1653, and to Samuel Clapp in 1690. Also a saw mill on 3d Herring Brook, belonging to Constant Clapp. The name of Clapp is given in Deane's History as one of thirteen families "most actively engaged in ship-building." Ship-builders by this name have gone from here to Medford, Mass., Bath, Me., and other places.

The Rev. Mr. Chauncey was minister of the first parish in Scituate, having been settled in 1641. He "would baptize only by immersion." This was warmly discussed throughout New England. Mr. Chauncey requested his opponents to refrain from coming to the communion. This led to the formation of a second church in 1642. The controversy terminated in 1675, having lasted 33 years. The Committee of Reconciliation consisted of Thomas Clapp and two others. The ability displayed in this discussion would do credit to any age.

In 1706 a larger meeting-house was required in that town, and Ensign Stephen Clapp and others were a committee to purchase land. A "Committee of Seaters, to appoint persons in which seat he or they shall sit in at the said meeting-house," was chosen. Lt. Stephen Clapp, one minister, two deacons, one captain, one private, constituted the committee.

1769, Voted to build a new meeting-house. Committee, Nathaniel Clapp, Galen Clapp, and two others.

1771, J. Jacobs and others petitioned the General Court to be set off. Nathaniel Clapp and two others were appointed "to make a representation." They did so, and the Committee reported against separation.

March 11, 1684, the town chose a Committee "to consider the general good—seriously of the premises and to impart their apprehensions to the town," consisting of Samuel Clapp and six others. They reported upon the *faithful and impartial administration of justice, exactness in financial matters, and in treasurer's accounts.*

May 27, 1686, the town met, the new book of laws being read, and "being desirous to prevent what may be hurtful," a Committee consisting of Thomas Clapp and others was appointed "to draw up our grievances, and impart their apprehensions to the town." This had reference to Sir Edmund Andros.

In 1787 the town chose a Committee (Constant Clapp and others) "to prepare instructions for their Representatives." They reported two pages of well prepared instructions.

The first Overseers of the Poor were Thomas Clapp and Charles Stockbridge.

In 1739, the town chose Capt. John Clapp and Samuel Clapp to "prosecute the law relative to the preservation and increase of deer." Capt. John Clapp was chosen annually for the same purpose until 1775, thirty-six years—and Constant Clapp was chosen annually afterwards until 1784. Here was an office conferred upon the same family for 45 years. It may well be questioned whether a parallel case can be found, at any period since the flood!

Thomas Clapp was Town Clerk in 1745; and Augustus Clapp, from 1799 to 1815. It so happens that Ebenezer Bailey, senior and junior, held the office of Town Clerk for a number of years. This might seem a little strange, were it not for the fact that the maiden name of their mother and grandmother was Abigail Clapp!

Cotton Mather commends a certain little book by Rev. Mr. Witherell, viz:—the "Life of John Clap of Scituate." This was a son of Thomas Clapp, remarkable for his understanding and his piety, and who died on his approach to manhood.

An anecdote is handed down in relation to this Mr. Witherell, who was Thomas Clapp's pastor. A parishioner had entered meeting late, and Mr. Witherell, at the close of his prayer, thus addressed him:—"Neighbor Bryant, it is to your reproach that you have disturbed the worship by entering late, living as you do within a mile of this place, and especially so, since here is goody Barstow, who has milked seven cows, made a cheese and walked five miles to the house of God in good season." Such is a specimen of the plainness and frankness in which the old and young of our name were trained in those days.

The Clapps of the town of Scituate bore a part in the French War; and appear also to have shown much activity in the Revolutionary War. On the town record in March, 1774, we find—"It was put whether the town would act upon the request of William Clapp, and others, touching the difficulties of the present times, and passed in the affirmative." A Committee of eleven was appointed, and among them Nathaniel Clapp, Esq., Galen Clapp, and John Clapp, jr. They made a report, filled with the spirit of those times.

October, 1774, "It was put whether the town would choose a Committee of Inspection, to see that the Continental Association shall be strictly adhered to," and passed. Galen Clapp, Increase Clapp, Samuel Clapp and Constant Clapp were on the Committee.

Committees of "Correspondence," of "Inspection," on "forming a State Constitution," of "Safety," on "Raising Minute Men," &c., were appointed, on all of which this family were represented.

In short, the Scituate branch of the family show a good record.

Northampton was organized as a town in 1654. It was represented in the Legislature in 1663. As it has never published a town history, its records are not easily accessible. The Legislature granted the town land for a village, provided twenty able and honest persons, householders, will engage to settle upon the same; and provided, always, that they take due care to provide preaching, &c. Sergeant Preserved Clapp was appointed, by the Legislature, one of a Committee to have charge of the same.

The records of the General Court show that Capt. Preserved Clapp was a member of that body from Northampton, in 1697, 1704, 1705 and 1708.

Easthampton was incorporated in 1785. The first district meeting was held at the house of Capt. Joseph Clapp. The first church was also organized in the same house. Thaddeus Clapp was Deacon of the church 33 years.

From 1785 to 1866, the Clapps had served in the board of Selectmen 26 years; Town Clerk, 21 years; School Committee, 7 years out of 40; and Representatives, 10 years out of 55.

Similar results occurred in other places, but I cannot give the details for want of access to the records.

When the British evacuated Boston, in 1776, they spiked, with rat-tail files, the cannon of the old Castle commanded by Roger Clap a century previous. Whether the old gentleman attempted to resent this aggression in his grave, history does not inform us. At any rate, his great-great-grandson, Preserved Clapp, descendant of Preserved of Northampton, an ingenious clock-maker, invented a hollow drill, by which the obstructions were removed. The grandson of this clock-maker—the venerable Derastus Clapp—is here present. This work was done by order of the Legislature, as will be seen by the following, copied from the Massachusetts State Records:—

"Memorial of Preserved Clap, overseer of the men employed in opening the Cannon at Boston, and Castle William. Setting forth—That he and the men attended that service for the term of time specified, for which he, nor they, have received any pay, therefore the memorialist prays that the Honorable Court would give him an order upon the

Treasurer of the State aforesaid for the amount of his account, or otherwise relieve him as shall seem meet."

"The Committee to whom was referred the consideration of the petition of Preserved Clap have attended that service, and beg leave to report by way of resolve."

"*Resolve on the Petition of Preserved Clap.* (Sept. 16, 1776, p. 263, v. 35.) *Resolved*, that there be paid out of the Public Treasury of this State to Preserved Clap, £43. 1*s.* 10*d.* in full for his account. And whereas said Clap says that he has invented a Machine for boring Cannon, which may be improved to the great advantage of this State, therefore Resolved, that if said *Clap* will exhibit a Plan or Model of said machine to Hugh Orr, Esq. and others, a Committee for casting large Cannon, so as to satisfy them of its Superior utility, upon their Report thereof to this Court, there shall then be granted to him such a sum for his invention as may appear adequate to its superior usefulness." (Resolves, Sep. 16, '76, p. 75.)

In conclusion, I will observe that it is not easy to so analyze the race of Clapps as to do them full justice. They seem to me, as a whole, to be quite a matter-of-fact, utilitarian class; not much given to the mere poetic, ideal, or transcendental. Their studies and pursuits have seemed to run more into the physical and actual, than into the sentimental or speculative. Hence we find them, in early as well as in later days, devoting themselves to farming, milling, tanning, ship-building, trading, manufacturing, and mechanical employments; preferring the useful to the useless—holding the doctrine that virtue is founded in utility—or that it is defined and enforced by its tendency to promote the highest happiness of humanity. They have seemed to regard the church, and civil government, when administered in the spirit of Divine Justice, as the main instrument to accomplish these ends. Their work in the past, we can contemplate with satisfaction. Not that there have been no speckled, or even black sheep in the flock. But still, few families have contributed to society a less number of loafers, vagabonds, or criminals.

But, finally, what are the duties which belong to the future? All empires, races, and families, go to decay, which fail in performing the duties which Providence has placed before them. Our duties would seem to be to aid in finishing the work which our fathers so well commenced. Let us therefore here renew our vows, and let each one for himself, and herself, embody in life the Golden Rule—the Divine basis for both Church and State.

What is the cause of the present convulsions in Europe? They are caused, in my judgment, by attempts to suppress those underlying principles, which brought our fathers to this wilderness for a resting place, more than two hundred years ago—viz., the rights of man as man, under the Divine Law. We are told, through the prophet, that "I will overturn, overturn, until He whose *right it is, shall reign.*" Divine Justice must and will reign in its *own right*, until it gives peace and comfort to all, through conformity to the Golden Rule. Man has only to overcome, through Divine aid, all inverted influences—the mob within himself—when *his millennium* will begin. The Puritans made a beginning—a most important and successful one—in this direction, and tasted some of its first fruits. Our duty lies in the same direction, and woe will be unto us if we fail in that duty.

THE dinner hour having arrived, an adjournment took place, with the not very comforting announcement that the unexpectedly large numbers which had congregated would render it impossible for more than half of them to be seated at the dinner table at once. This necessarily interfered with the original plan of making that the place for a more social and familiar mingling of all who might be present at the family gathering. The only remedy was to meet again in the large hall in the afternoon to transact any business that might be brought up, to listen to such speeches and papers as might have been prepared, and still further to bring together and make acquainted the scattered members of the family —so many of whom then met each other for the first time.

At the afternoon meeting, the following resolution was offered and passed unanimously:—

Whereas, our kinsman, Ebenezer Clapp, Esq., of Dorchester, has devoted many years' labor to collecting the genealogy of Roger, Edward, Nicholas, Thomas, and John Clapp, the first emigrants of their name, and their descendants; and

Whereas, It seems very desirable that such work should be made as perfect as possible by completing all the family records of their descendants, and bringing them down to the present time, therefore

Resolved, That a committee of three be nominated by the chair to coöperate with Mr. E. Clapp, in completing and preparing the work for the press, and also in printing and publishing the same. Otis Clapp, William B. Trask, and David Clapp, all of Boston, were appointed on the committee.

A subscription list for the work was circulated through the hall, and the following committee appointed to procure further subscriptions: H. N. Rust of Easthampton, Albert S. Clapp of Deerfield, Charles Clapp of Wethersfield, Conn., W. C. Clapp of Dorchester, Martin H. Clapp of Montague, S. E. Bridgman of Northampton, Joel T. Clapp of Southampton, Alexander Clapp of Windsor, Conn., J. B. Clapp of Hartford, Alfred Clapp of Huntington, and Dr. Sylvanus Clapp of Pawtucket.

The President announced that circumstances would prevent the calling upon individuals, as was intended, to speak as representatives of the respective branches of the family, and he should therefore request Deacon EBENEZER CLAPP, of Dorchester, who was now well known to the audience as the family historian, to say a few words in behalf of the descendants of Roger, Edward and Nicholas, he claiming a lineal descent from each of these three progenitors. Deacon C. then read a paper which he had prepared, as follows:—

KINSMEN AND FRIENDS:

We are all curious to know something of our progenitors, of those who preceded us on this stage of action; especially is it interesting to learn about those who first landed on these shores—an event which has proved to be one of the most important in the world's history. After an interesting study for thirty years of the large and growing family before me, it gives me great pleasure to see so many of you together. It seems but a short time since the origin of our country; but how rapidly history has developed itself during these two hundred and fifty years! Its growth in that time corresponds with that of the older nations in two thousand years; its events "have chased one another down like the generations of men;" its civilization has travelled westward, like an advancing army on its march; its cities and towns have sprung up in rapid succession, till the well-known phrase "Westward the star of empire takes its way" has lost its significance; the national banner has been unfurled on our western coast, and henceforth civilization must travel Eastward.

I go back in imagination to the days and circumstances that made, or founded, the Puritan party, among whom were our ancestors. Time will permit me to speak but very briefly of its history. Suffice it to say, they declined to submit their faith to any human authority, or to transfer to others their right of private judgment on matters of faith; a faith that was really the "substance of things hoped for, the evidence of things not seen." They had an unbounded hostility both to Church and State as exemplified in the mother country; and held themselves responsible in spiritual matters to God alone. This dislike grew by persecution into a dogged obstinacy. We read their records, written in sincerity and truth, and learn of their hopes, their fears, their discouragements and their sorrows; we also learn of their resolves, and their fortitude, which put under foot all minor difficulties. Yet they came into a wilderness. It was not home, nor a country; "both were to be created."

My reading and observation for many years have led me into a study of the Puritan character; and I am impressed with admiration at its wonderful significance. Made into a sect or party by oppression and abuse, they grew strong, and stamped their age by their wonderful achievements. No terrors could fright, no honors or rewards tempt them; they cared not to have their names registered in the "book of heralds," anxious only that they might be recorded in the "book of life." Archbishop Laud could not lure them by his introduction of Sunday sports; nor deter them from following their deliberate judgment, by silencing four hundred of their ministers. I hold that the Puritans, as a class, party, or sect, whichever they may be denominated, acted up to their convictions. Some of those convictions, we may believe, were rigid and unreasonable, and associated with the party must have been some hard and selfish men; but they and their descendants have been in the front rank of all that has tended to advance civilization, intelligence, industry, ingenuity, intellect, and the rights of man; their virtues predominated over their faults, amid every pressure of adversity. They were as shrewd, vigilant, and far-seeing, as politicians, as they were earnest and sincere in their religious belief. These opinions I hold of their spirit, character and mission, without sympathizing with many of their peculiar and now outgrown ideas.

Let the fault-finders and traducers of the Puritans rail on; they cannot deceive the faithful expounders of history, nor arrest the progress of their descendants, so long as they hold to the Bible, that essential platform of their progenitors. "I am verily persuaded," said the renowned John Robinson (in his parting address to the Pilgrims), "that the Lord has more truth yet to break forth from his holy Word." As this truth has been revealed, they have embraced and acknowledged it; and perhaps no sect, party, religion, or community, are without leading men from among them. The light of the 19th century must not be the standard of the 17th; to so compare and judge, is an act of manifest injustice.

In the past it is plain that no danger could subdue, no trouble conquer the men who first settled this land: if in the future their posterity fall, wealth and luxury will be the means; these are the snares that overcome, undermine or extinguish a people. But we hope and believe of them better things. There is much work for them yet to do; there are many lands to be explored, many truths to be acknowledged, many inventions to be made, and many oppressions to be overturned. In the words of another, "It is for them to search creation through, climb all mountains, cross and sound all seas; number, classify, and follow in their course all the stars of the firmament; dig into the bowels of the earth, gather its hidden treasures, fathom every secret, solve every riddle of nature, copy all beauty, breathe all music, and accumulate for use and enjoyment whatever of comfort or of luxury nature can supply."

And now, my friends, I have not said a word in relation to our own lineage; there is not time for that here. That they have contributed their full share in bringing this country to its present condition, I cannot doubt; that they and their descendants will coöperate till this bright picture is realized, I am equally confident.

This is an occasion I had not expected to witness, and one that I shall not forget. Let us all look forward with bright hope and anticipation to the time, when Roger, and Edward, and Thomas, and Nicholas, and John, with all their descendants, shall be gathered into the Kingdom eternal, and become sharers in its unspeakable blessings.

JOHN CLAPP, Esq., of Binghamton, N. Y., was now introduced by the President of the Day, and made the following speech, the lively humor of which was well received by the audience :—

MR. PRESIDENT, AND KINDRED :—

After what you have listened to, does anything remain, which I can say, to instruct you, or even to amuse? Nothing, absolutely nothing, so thoroughly has everything been done. I can only express my surprise, as well as pleasure, in being made acquainted with this large number of relatives, heretofore unknown to me. So profound was my ignorance of my family, whence it came, or who its members, that I scarcely knew the names of my father and mother; but you will pardon me for not being accquainted with them, when you know that both died before my age had reached a single year. I never met with but one individual stranger, bearing the name of "Clapp," until I was so fortunate as to be discovered by the "Historian," since which time I have seen several of the name.

I am under great obligations to this "Historian," who found me, by examining a list of Postmasters, during the reign of John McLean, of honest memory! Emerging from the vale of the beautiful Chenango, I visited the "Historian," and soon found out that my father's name was Thomas, and my grandfather's Roger. My library was enlarged, and I began to study the "Memoirs of Capt. Roger Clap."

The moment the "Historian" put his eyes on me, he said, "I know where you come from; you belong to the black branch of the family." And you see he was right on that point, as he always is. The more I studied the "Memoirs," the more satisfied I became with my relatives. I began to feel well acquainted with Capt. Roger and his charming little family, especially the young ladies Elizabeth, Experience, Wait, Waitstill, Hopestill, Thanks, Desire, Unite—and Supply, and Tom, and the other boys. Think of the blessings of a family circle, ye modern brides! Possibly, some of these young ladies may have been masculine, as they are named amongst the Ruling Elders. But I do not consider this conclusive; as women, about the days of the "May Flower," had something to say, as well as to do, besides dressing for the Opera or the Church!

As I have said, I studied the Memoirs of my great ancestor, and noticed some things which were interesting, to which, please permit me to allude. The voyage over occupied about seventy days, with the usual horrors and perils of the ocean, in a great ship of 400 tons, bigger than any canal boat, but not as large as the Great Eastern! The tedium was brightened by expounding the Gospel "every day for ten weeks." Think of that, you who worship in fashionable churches; for the preaching was not after the style of the Rev. Morphine Velvet, but brought the bottomless pit plainly into view, as the doom of the unconverted!

The "Tremont House" was not then built, so that it was difficult to obtain good board, at a reasonable price. Food was scanty. Roger remarks, "Many a time, if I could have filled my belly, tho' with mean victuals, it would have been sweet unto me. And when I could have *meal* and *water* and *salt*, boiled together, it was so good, who could wish better?" Think of dining with Roger, and then think of the tables, groaning with abundance, from which we have just arisen!

Roger and his companions soon manifested their love of trade and "swapping," now so marked a characteristic of a New Englander. We are not informed as to "whittling." They generally "whittled" Indians, not having plenty of shingles. One of his greatest trades was a "*swap*" with an Indian, Roger giving a "puppy dog" for a peck of corn. It was a fair trade, as no complaint was made by either party, so it is probable the Indian had a good dinner.

My friends, these little things, which appear so ludicrous, point unmistakably to terrible destitution and suffering, for want of food.

Roger left much good advice for his children; for instance, "*Watch over your ears.*" Possibly, this was in consequence of his having been present at a little performance in 1631, when a noisy fellow, who *spoke against the Government, had both ears cut off.* This was done in Boston, and Roger says, "I saw it done."

They were temperate men in those days. As early as 1632, it was discovered that a Mr. Allen had "*aboute* 2. *gallandes*" of strong water, which the Court, very considerately, ordered taken from him, to be delivered to the "*Deacons of Dorchester,*" for the benefit of the poor; meaning, I suppose, those who were not able to buy their drinks. Perhaps this was the origin of the "Maine Law."

Notwithstanding so much that seems quaint, narrow, prejudiced, bitter, even cruel, you must remember, my friends, these were the errors of the times. In the reign of Queen Elizabeth, near two hundred offences against the law were punished capitally. Sir Matthew Hale was willing to preside over a trial for witchcraft! Light was just breaking over Europe; and perhaps, in no portion of the earth at that time, was greater security found for life, property and conscience, than with the little band of emigrants who clustered around one another in the shadow of the forest, looking to God alone for protection.

Nothing can exceed the beauty and sublimity of the dying words of our majestic, grand old progenitor to his children! "And now, dear children, I know not the time of my death; my time is in God's hands; but my age shows it cannot be far off. I do charge you solemnly—Fear the Lord our God, and obey his commandments. See that you fear Him, and stand in awe and *sin not.* If you do truly love God, you will keep all his commandments, and you will *hate evil.* Strive to live in Love and Peace with all men. Be courteous—Be sober—Be charitable—Set your affections on things above, not on things below; not on Riches, Honors and Pleasures."

Such, my friends, were some of the dying words of Roger Clap! What can be added? What more, or rather, what *wiser words* will you hear, from the pulpits of the day, shaken with the very thunder of modern preaching!

I am proud of my descent from such a stock, and happy in the acquaintance I have made of this great family of relatives. May we come together again, and find as now no stain on the family escutcheon; and let us all unite in the motion, which, Mr. President, I now make, that the thanks of this assemblage be tendered to the gentlemen who conceived the idea of this gathering, and who have so successfully hunted up, and brought together, this wide-spread, numerous and happy family.

The motion was put to vote by the President, and carried unanimously.

SYLVANUS CLAPP, M.D., of Pawtucket, R. I., being called upon as a representative of the Medical Profession, read the following paper:—

It is fitting, and preëminently so, that we the descendants of those men who have done so much to give to New England her character and history, from its earliest period to the present time, should honor their memories, and reproduce in our own lives those virtues which adorned their earthly career. In doing this, it is their character as well as their deeds that we love to recall and cherish. And when I remember the aged men bearing the name of Clapp living in my boyhood days, those I loved and reverenced, I now feel that they were the men who had passed the dangers and temptations of life safe and complete; and I do not wonder I so loved and admired them. I might call them by name, but they are remembered by many of us as the public and useful men of the towns of Northampton, Southampton, Easthampton, Westhampton, Pittsfield, Worthington, Chesterfield and Belchertown. They made an impression on my mind which will never be erased until my earth-life ends.

It is such men who have given to New England its character. They never sacrificed principle to self-interest; but always first considered whether it was right to do this or that, and acted accordingly. Principle was always paramount to personal interest with them.

They were earnest, conscientious, self-reliant men. They pushed aside difficulties that surprised men of less energetic character.

When you find men of such earnest spirit, combined with such prudence and caution as they possessed, you find men of great influence in the world. They did not spend their time in defending the truth only; but they *exemplified* and *lived* the truth. They were industrious men. They used their talents, whether great or small. They have not been the men who said they had no place in the world.

This has been true of our women, as well as men:—And there is one such among us to-day, whose girlhood days were spent in this town. Her heart was always full of good and noble deeds, always the most happy when doing the most good. She found a place in our army, and like Florence Nightingale ministered to the wants of our wounded and sick soldiers, until smitten with disease, and came near laying down her own life for the good of others. Such lives always produce good results. Such influence and usefulness are never wasted, but live on amidst all the mutations of human life.

I consider I should do injustice to the present occasion, if I did not speak of the life and character of one of my earliest playmates and a life-long friend—the Rev. Dexter Clapp. We were as brothers; born within a few months of each other, living in the same neighborhood, and enjoying all the pleasures of our youthful days together, it is not strange we should have so loved each other.

The following notice of his life and death, taken from one of the public papers, well describes the loveliness of his character:—

"It is with sorrow that we record the departure of another faithful worker and devoted spirit from the earthly field and fold. Rev. Dexter Clapp was born in Westhampton, Mass., July 15, 1816, and graduated at Amherst in 1839. After fitting himself for the ministry, to which he felt himself called at an early period, at the Cambridge Divinity School, he preached for a time at Deerfield, Mass., but declined a settlement in order to accept a call from the society in Savannah, Ga., over which he was ordained in November, 1843. There he remained about two years and a half, working with great fidelity and preaching with acceptance and fervor until his health yielded to the influence of the climate and the drain of incessant labor upon his never strong constitution. Returning to the North, he was immediately invited to settle over the Church in West Roxbury, whose pulpit had been vacated by the removal of Mr. Parker to Boston, and was installed as its minister in December, 1846. The steadiness of his course, the sweetness of his spirit, the beauty of his quiet, active, useful life and Christian character, made a profound impression on all who knew him, while his discourses, though never brilliant, but always thoughtful, serious and full of unction, made his ministry here quite successful. In 1851 he accepted a call from the East Church in Salem, to become the colleague of the venerable Dr. Flint, and was installed December 17 of that year. Here he remained ten years, when the failure of his health made it necessary for him to sever a relation which was almost sacred in its sweetness and intimacy. Since that time he has struggled against his disease or borne its pain and weariness with quiet, manly Christian fortitude and resignation. For a time last winter his health seemed to improve, and he went South, stopping on his way home in this city. But the consumption was too deeply seated to yield, and at last his physical frame was overcome by its ceaseless wear and waste. At last, on Sunday, July 27, he passed on. So lived and wrought and suffered and passed away one of the most pure-minded, single-hearted, meek, devout, consecrated spirits we have ever known—a true saint, if such an one ever walked the world, and one whose memory itself is a benediction and a sanctity. It is hard to part with such as these, but it is a joy to think that what earth loses heaven will gain."

I take the liberty, also, to quote from two letters I received a few days after his death—one written to Rev. Dr. (now Bishop) Huntington, by Rev. Rufus Ellis, D.D., the other by Rev. Dr. Huntington to myself. Dr. Ellis writes:—

"The dear, good, sweet fellow! He strove bravely to the end, only during the last he said that his time was coming, and yielded in all faith, hope, and love. They told me nothing could exceed his patience and gentle submission; that his body of flesh seemed to fall away from him and leave the spirit free to see the visions of the heavenly city. He expressed, as you may well know, the strongest love for you his life-long friend. He looked calm and grave and bright in his last rest, and you would have rejoiced to have gazed upon him even so. It is hard to give him up, even for a short time. There are not many such for us. There was something so inexpressibly winning in all that he was. I think he had come at last to the conclusion that life in this world was no longer to be desired. The hope of being any more of service in his chosen work died out at last, and he looked the other way, and was more than content. I can hardly think that so much is lost out of my earthly future."

The Rev. Dr. Huntington, in his letter addressed to me, says:—

"Thirty-five years ago I began to know and love him, at Hopkins Academy. We were chums four years; and almost that, three years more, and our hearts I am sure were never divided. I have always regarded him as the most amiable of all the men I ever knew. His cheery, buoyant, unselfish, affectionate nature, made an atmosphere of harmony and peace, wherever he was. We are all made mourners by the departure of so much goodness:—but it lives elsewhere."

A Committee of three, consisting of ELBRIDGE CLAPP of Quincy, HIRAM CLAPP of Dorchester, and JOHN B. CLAPP of Hartford, was appointed to confer respecting the time and place for holding another Family Gathering.

After singing Auld Lang Syne, the meeting adjourned—some of the members to remain for a time in the neighborhood, others returning at once to their homes, and all carrying with them increased knowledge of the names and history of their ancestors, and a stronger attachment than ever before to the whole family whose first gathering had now so happily terminated.

OTHER papers had been prepared for the occasion, but circumstances interfered with their being read. Among them was the following, by JOHN CODMAN CLAPP, Esq., of Cambridge.—A sentiment, from another source, is also appended, which doubtless embodies the feeling of a large number present towards a place so hallowed in all our memories as the ancient town of Dorchester.

Perhaps few of the *Million-heirs* of Capt. Roger Clap are ever likely to be *Millionaires.* Suppose they are not. Think of the man in Scripture who thought to satisfy the desires of his soul out of his full stored barns, and plentiful grounds, and what he was called. Artemus Ward says, "There is many a person who kan sit a mouse trap two perfection, but not satisfied with sich small game, undertake two sit a trap for bears, and get ketched by the bears. Moral—Study your genius, and stick to mice." And yet, I don't know that the Clapps have, or should have stuck to small game. They are a thinking, active, industrious, honest people, endeavoring to fulfil the great destinies of life, and have been enabled to make their *mark* in the world, whether they could write or not. Some have occupied the higher positions in life. Look at the history of Dorchester; see the names strewed thickly among its lists of officers. Many have been honored as officers in the church as well as in civil life. To say Deacon Clapp, in Dorchester, a few years ago, did not designate any one, as there were five there who held that title at the same time. As far as I can learn, a less number have been of vicious or intemperate habits than those of other names.

Is there not a great truth underlying this, which is contained in the second commandment—I the Lord thy God am a jealous God, visiting the iniquities of the fathers upon the children to the third and fourth generation of them that *hate* me, and showing mercy to *thousands* of them that *love* me and keep my commandments. Now every one who has read Capt. Roger Clap's memoirs knows that the great thought of his life was, that his children, the colony, the world, should become holy, in order that they might become happy. No wonder he raised a holy generation to follow him; it is a natural consequence; we are living not only to form our own characters, but also to mould that of our children, and children's children. He was a godly man, and with his family were constant hearers of the word preached, when in command of the Castle, though it was about four miles to church.

I have thought that his spirit might be hovering over us now, saying, in the words of John in his third Epistle: "I have no greater joy than to know that my children walk in the truth."

DORCHESTER—good old Dorchester—older than Boston or Cambridge or Charlestown—the home of Roger Clap and his brethren—the birthplace of his son Preserved, the Captain, Ruling Elder, and Representative of Northampton—the birthplace since of Everett and many other worthies; although now absorbed into the great neighboring metropolis, its name shall not die with its corporate existence, but be handed down to future generations associated with the names and virtues of its early settlers.

The following extract from a letter written by a lady in one of the distant western States, to a kinsman in Boston, may be taken as a specimen of the interest felt in the late gathering by many of the family who were unavoidably absent:

"Dear Friend,

"I wish you knew how much pleasure I experience in saying 'Dear Friend,' remote as I am from kindred; fatherless, having buried my husband, my father-in-law, my mother-in-law, also a dear little niece quite recently. This new kinship, and the pleasing reminiscences growing out of it, seem a sort of compensating solace to one who looks for help to bear heavy griefs. I hoped, until the last moment, to be able to meet the hundreds of our family who gathered at Northampton; but my heart, certainly, was there, and I perused with eager interest the account you sent me, for which please accept my thanks. It seemed like reading a letter from home. I fancy that our ancestry upon the other side of the 'beautiful river' must have been present; and who knows how every noble purpose, every self-sacrificing spirit of the gathered throng may have been strengthened and buoyed up by the ministering spirits present there? This may be but an idle fancy, but quite natural, I think. I shall be pleased to receive a copy of the pamphlet containing an account of the meeting."

The annexed ancient letter, from the Rev. Supply Clap, of Woburn, Mass., to Rev. Nathaniel Clap, of Newport, R. I., will be read with interest. Some notice of the minister last named will be found in the Address, page 25. The letter is taken from Vol. xv. of the *N. E. Hist. and Genealogical Register*, into which periodical it was copied verbatim from the original, furnished by Mr. William B. Trask, of Dorchester.

Wob: Decr 25th 1742.

Rev^{d}: Father,

I received a Little bottle from you, the contents of wch I took; which (by ye Divine blessing) I hope was serviceable to me. I thank you for it. I have been (according to ye Good will of a holy God) bro't to ye Gates of ye Grave, w^{n} I tho't I should be deprived of ye residue of my years. But when near departing, as myself and others apprehended, God was ready to save, Jehovah-jireh, God appeared in ye mount of Difficulty and I am returned to see ye Lord in ye Land of ye Living and to behold man again. I am still a poor weak Creature, as I have often heard you say of yourself. I have many painfull Days and restless nights. I hope God intends all for my Good and y[t] I shall Learn humility, Patience, resignation to Gods will &c: in this School of affliction. I make no doubt I have had your prayers for me, I ask them still. My family is in good health, by Gods Goodness. My wife sends her Duty to you. We have two Children, Martha and Supply, pray God to bless them and make y[m] blessings. My Love and Service to Mr Gardner. Now wishing Grace mercy and peace may be multiplied to you and y[e] flock to whom you have so long been made a blessing, and asking y[r] prayers for a blessing on me and my flock, I subscribe myself, y[r] Dutifull tho' unworthy Son in y[e] Ministry.

SUPPLY CLAP.

P. S. I heard from Dorchester, not long since. Our friends and Relations w[re] in good health generally. There is a Little number y[t] hold a Separate meeting yet on Lords Days. It is remarkable, That y[re] hath not been one Exhorter among my people yet, we are in peace, (God grant it may not be a peace and Security in Sinning.)

I beg y[e] out pouring of Gods Spirit on my people and upon y[e] Land, and that God would preserve his people from Errors, which I fear are many at this Day. I trust we must still, To y[e] Law and to y[e] Testimonies, Stick to y[e] Bible and make Gods word our Rule. Please to write to me by y[e] first opportunity, That I may hear (I hope) of y[r] welfare and receive your blessing in y[e] Lord. S. CLAP.

For the Rev[d]
M[r] Nathaniel Clap
Pastor of a C[hh] in Newport
on Road-Island
These

Rev. Supply Clap was son of Samuel and Mary, born in Dorchester, June 1, 1711; grandson of Elder Samuel, and great-grandson of Capt. Roger. He graduated at Harvard College in 1731; taught school several years, and was ordained pastor of the 2d Church in Woburn, Oct. 29, 1735. He was a man of feeble health, which was a great interruption to his pulpit services. He died Dec. 28, 1747, in the 37th year of his age. Rev. Samuel Sewall, one of his successors, says of him: "Not a syllable has been handed down to us to his disadvantage." He was present at the New South Church in Boston, in 1740, at the time when the Rev. Mr. Whitefield preached and there was an outcry that the galleries were falling, causing a rush of people to the doors. Mr. C. assisted in clearing the door-way, and helping out the wounded. Three persons were killed upon the spot, and two died a day or two after.

The undersigned—a Committee appointed at the late Clapp Family Meeting to coöperate with Mr. Ebenezer Clapp in the completion and publication of the family genealogy upon which he has expended much time and labor—take this opportunity to solicit the still further coöperation of those of the name and kindred who have not yet furnished all the information in their power towards making the work as complete as possible up to the present time. Blanks will be supplied for the record of names and dates in the shape most desirable. Those who have subscribed for the book must not of course expect its immediate publication. An early attention to the above request will expedite its preparation for the press.

The Committee are authorized by those having charge of the printing of this pamphlet to say that any pecuniary profits from its sale will be passed to the credit of the genealogy book above alluded to.

Otis Clapp,
William B. Trask,
David Clapp.

www.ingramcontent.com/pod-product-compliance
Lightning Source LLC
Chambersburg PA
CBHW021519090426
42739CB00007B/686

* 9 7 8 3 7 4 4 6 9 2 7 5 5 *